With a BA in psychology and postgraduate work in transpersonal studies, Sharon Klingler was originally inspired to investigate greater consciousness as a result of her profound experiences as an identical twin. Now well known in the media throughout America and the South Pacific, Sharon Klingler is a leading inter-national Intuitive who has run a busy and successful private practice for more than twenty-five years, with high-profile clients from all around the world

Intuition
and Beyond

Intuition
and
Beyond

A Step-By-Step Approach to
Discovering Your Inner Voice

Sharon A. Klingler

RIDER
LONDON • SYDNEY • AUCKLAND • JOHANNESBURG

9 10

First published in 2002 by Rider,
an imprint of Ebury Press, Random House
20 Vauxhall Bridge Road, London SW1V 2SA

www.randomhouse.co.uk

The Random House Group Limited Reg. No. 954009

A CIP catalogue record for this book
is available from the Britsh Library

ISBN 9780712634427

The Random House Group Limited supports The Forest Stewardship
Council® (FSC®), the leading international forest-certification organisation.
Our books carrying the FSC label are printed on FSC®-certified paper.
FSC is the only forest-certification scheme supported by the leading
environmental organisations, including Greenpeace. Our
paper procurement policy can be found at
www.randomhouse.co.uk/environment

Printed and bound in Great Britain by Clays Ltd, St Ives plc

CONTENTS

*This book is dedicated with great love
to my husband, Rudy,
my father, Ronald,
and my grandfather, Charlie –
the men in my spirit-life*

Acknowledgements

My deepest appreciation and gratitude go to the following:

Those who helped me edit this book: Ed Coughanor, Barbara Van Rensselaer, Julianne Stein and Julia McCutchen. Thank you for sharing my dream and your vision.

My wonderful family: Devin Staurbringer, my dear son and kindred spirit; Sarah Klingler, my devoted and generous mother; Anna Salvaggio, my grandmother and inspiration; Sandra Taylor, my eternal twin and her husband Benjamin; Vica and Jenyaa, my niece and nephew of joy; Grandma Yvonne and Grandpa Earl; my other son, Jeremiah Freedman, and his wife Deanna (my new daughter!); my brothers and sisters of home and heart, Kevin and Kathryn Klingler, Marilyn Verbus, Thomas Bagiackas and Melissa Matousek; and, finally, Carol, Rosie and Adam Staubringer, my second family.

My colleagues and friends: Tom Cratsley, Donna Eden, Ellie McCabe Cratsley, John C. White, Susan and Jeff Salkin, Barbara Freedman Bagiackas, Tim Brainard, Saundra Cortese, Lalei Gutierrez, Michael Freedman, Loren Schuh and Dr George Berki – all of them extraordinary counsellors, mediums and healers.

My friends and advocates around the globe: Graham Wilson, Valerie Darville, Graeme Lloyd, Avram Gold, Ros Burton and Derek Leach – your love and support have literally meant the world to me.

EVERYONE in the Lily Dale family – especially Sue Glasier and Joanne Taft for your tireless efforts for our community; Joyce LaJudice for keeping the history of Lily Dale alive; Paula Vogt for chronicling parts of that history in text; John Goldsby and all those whose love and hard work make Lily Dale thrive. (Lily Dale, New York, is the largest and oldest spiritualist community and education centre in the United States.)

Rhonda Lamvermeyer, a computing genius; and Clarice Bronako, angel-accountant.

Each and every client, student and meditation group member

x

– you have shared nothing less than your spirit and consequently have opened the doors to heaven.

All those who have given their great assistance with an open heart: Linda Smigel, Richard Pietz, Ted Henry, Dennis Kucinich, Lynda Hirsch, Linda Huffman Hayes, Mark and Andrea Abushady, Allison Abner, Linda Villarosa, Emmy Chetkin, Caroline Favale, Nancy Koran, Mary Matusz, Annemarie Osborne, Julie Stillman, Shelly Takei, Garry Wiseman, Andrea Loushine, Jenny Danko, Tony and Sharon Drew, Clara Villarosa, Vincent Favale, Robert Goulet and June Marsh Lazar.

And, finally, the Divine Spirit above who lives in each and every one of us. May we follow that spirit now and forever.

* * * * *

Part I

Looking into Intuition

What's In(tu)it
for You?

Be a listener only ...
And endeavor to establish with yourself
the habit of silence.

— Thomas Jefferson

1

Looking into Intuition

What do you want? Do you want to create abundance and financial freedom? Do you want to discover a greater purpose in life and a more abiding peace? Would you like to recognise the best opportunities and people at the very moment they present themselves to you? Do you want to be more successful at choosing the right people in your personal and professional relationships? Perhaps you would like to improve your health and sense of well-being. Or maybe you would just like a clearer idea of what it is you want!

Assuming that you would like to make all of these discoveries and become the best you can be, there is only one professional alive who can help you achieve these goals. You! Yes, there's an expert inside you who has the skills to help you in every endeavour in your life. And this expert is your spirit. Though this professional has always been available to you, you haven't always recognised its voice and haven't always heeded its advice. But don't despair; even though this inner voice is silent, you can learn to listen to it.

As the Good Witch of the North says at the end of *Wizard of Oz*, 'You've always had it in you, Dorothy!' And, like Dorothy, *you* can find the truth and power inside *you*. Then you, too, will discover how truly to get home!

Deep in the soul, everybody has the answer.

– Leo Tolstoy

Intuition – a Rose by Many Other Names

You have probably heard a dozen different terms describing the concept of 'intuition'. You may call it instinct, second sight, a gut feeling, an inner voice, your sixth sense, or even your soul. Whatever you call it, you have the opportunity to experience it every single day and use it to benefit your life and your world.

The dictionary defines intuition as 'direct knowing or learning of something without the conscious use of reasoning'. Clinical parapsychologists have defined this 'knowing' as the perceiving of information without the use of the *physical* senses (hence, the term 'extrasensory perception'). They have determined it to be a function belonging to the vast 'unused' portion of the brain. Still others (myself included) see it as the voice of our eternal (and consequently divine) self, our spirit. And, finally, those who wish to stay away from the more philosophical, clinical, spiritual or even technical interpretations simply call any intuitive experience 'a hunch'.

In this book you will find a number of terms used interchangeably; the following are used frequently:

- Intuitive voice (or intuition) = the voice of spirit
- Ego = the temporary or material self (or the personal mind)
- Spirit (or soul) = the permanent self; eternal (or divine) self

Though it may seem that looking into intuition can cause a good deal of confusion, it's only the actual *naming* of it that's confusing. *In truth, getting beyond the confusion in your life is one of the best reasons for using intuition.* Your intuition enables you to do this by providing you with a 'direct knowing', regardless of the many different (and often confusing, conflicting and sometimes misleading) sources of information in your life.

BREAK THROUGH

Right now your intuitive self is giving you (through an image or a feeling) a dictionary which contains the one word that reflects what intuition means to you (or what it can do for you). Close your eyes and open up this dictionary to find out what this word is. Trust the first thing you 'get', even if it may not make perfect sense. How does this word feel as a reflection of your inner voice? Would you like to enhance or make any changes to this defining word?

There is a being which exists in everything, and without which there is no heaven and no earth ... People try to describe its qualities, give it different names ... but the being itself has no names.

– Lao Tzu

These sources of information and opinion come in many forms and from many places, both internal and external. Everything – from your emotions to your logic, from your friends' persuasions to a professional's advice – seeks to influence your decisions. Unfortunately, these sources may not always provide the influence that will take you to your highest good.

One of the biggest sources of information in your life is your emotional self. Your emotions tell you how you feel and what fills (and hurts) your heart. Acceptance and understanding of your emotions are vitally important in order to know how your feelings motivate your life. Yet, while each and every emotion you have is valid and true for you, they don't always give you the insight you need when it's time to make important decisions. Indeed, your emotions can often deceive you about what may be best for you.

Conscious or unconscious memories of even a single traumatic event can be so painful that they may cause you to avoid a similar situation for the rest of your life. For instance, the pain you went through during your parents' divorce could make you determined never to marry. Or a small embarrassing moment in a school play could make you decide never to perform or speak before an audience again. In both of these situations (although to varying degrees), fear is keeping you from a potentially enriching activity that would be supported by your intuitive self.

Strongly emotional memories can affect you in many ways. Some people relive traumatic events over and over mentally, recreating in the present the events that caused fear or pain in the past. The great (and tortured alcoholic) American novelist, F. Scott Fitzgerald, offered significant evidence of this during an interview with reporter, Michel Mok. Between frequent trips across the room to refill his glass, Fitzgerald related the story of his father's ruin:

> One afternoon – I was ten or eleven – the phone rang and my mother answered it. I didn't understand what she said, but I felt that disaster had come to us. My mother, a little while before, had given me a quarter to go swimming. I gave the money back to her. I knew something terrible had happened and I thought she could not spare the money now.
>
> Then I began to pray. 'Dear God,' I prayed, 'please don't let us go to the poor house; please don't let us go to the poor house.' A little while later my father came home. He had lost his job.

> That morning he had gone out a comparatively
> young man, a man full of strength, full of confidence.
> He came home that evening, an old man, a completely
> broken man ... He was a failure the rest of his days ...
> My father lost his grip, and I lost my grip.[1]

Though Fitzgerald had been pacing the room during the telling of this story, he seemed to become even more agitated when the reporter asked him (in an attempt to change the subject for the better) about what he was working on now.

When a moment later Fitzgerald briefly left the room, his ever-present nurse leaned toward the interviewer and whispered, 'Despair, despair, despair. Despair day and night. Try not to talk about his work or his future.'

Though he had become a celebrated author, Fitzgerald's past not only haunted him, it defined him. And the emotions of fear and loss from his childhood became the voice that filled his present and lost him his future.

Another voice within you is that of your analytical mind. Like your emotional voice, this too is an important part of your life and should always be considered when making significant decisions. But (as with your emotions) it should not necessarily be the determining factor. Now, clearly, there are some situations where analysis of the facts can provide you with the answers you need. If you're shopping for a new house, for instance, and you've fallen in love with one that is way above your budget, you will obviously have to keep looking. Still, there are many situations in life where analysis of the pros and cons will only take you so far. After that you will find that your intuition will be your best guide.

Of course, there are several other factors in decision-making besides your emotions and logic. Your body can tell you which foods it will tolerate. Your lawyer can determine which contract would be best to sign. Your friends can tell you which person to date. Your broker can advise you on which stock to buy. And, last but not least, your mother will happily share her opinion about whom you should marry.

It is best (indeed, necessary) to consider all sources of information – your body, your emotions, your logic, and even others' advice – when making any important decision. Your emotions and all of your internal voices can lead you to a greater wisdom and understanding of yourself. (We will take a look at these different voices in Part II.) Yet, in the end you must always go back to your intuition for the answer.

As hotel magnate, Conrad Hilton, once said, 'I know when I have a problem and have done all I can – I keep listening in a sort of inside silence 'til something clicks and I feel a right answer.'[2]

No matter who you are or what the issue may be, somehow, some way, your intuitive mind will always tell you what's best for you – how you can realise your highest intention and greatest joy in life – if only you make the effort to listen.

Listening to this 'inside silence' may seem rather confusing when you have all of these other voices, opinions and distinct needs within you and around you. This book will help you learn how to listen to this inner voice more successfully, but you *have* heard this voice before. It has told you things that were helpful. It has told you things that you sometimes didn't want to hear.

If you look back over your life, you will recall that it was only when you went *against* your intuitive voice that you found yourself in the wrong place or with the wrong people, or engaged in an activity that eventually brought you unhappiness and sorrow. The *most* confusion you will ever experience will usually come as the result of *not* listening to your intuition. *And the most help that you will ever have will come to you because you did.*

How Intuition Can Work in Your Life

1. It helps you to recognise the best opportunities available to you and supports you in taking the action to embrace those opportunities, regardless of what your other sources of information and opinion say.

   When Oprah Winfrey first had the opportunity to move to Chicago, she says that she did so not because her common sense or her friends told her she should, but because her intuition directed her to go, in spite of the great risk involved in moving away from her established career and into an untested market. 'When you have finished growing in one place or time, you know. Your soul tells you when it's time to move on.'[3] The rest, of course, is history – still in the making!

2. It helps you make the best choices about relationships and about your actions within those relationships. (I have a client in New York City who was very hesitant to marry because of trust issues about sharing financial responsibility. But her inner voice wouldn't let her remain in fear. It led her to a happy marriage and an opportunity to work through her fears about security.)

3. It helps you make the right choices in financial matters (as in the case of Conrad Hilton, Cornelius Vanderbilt, and many others).

4. It helps you tap into a greater experience of your creativity. (In a poll of Nobel Prize-winning scientists, the majority said they believed intuition had been an important factor in their discoveries.)

5. It creates a better understanding of your sense of purpose and how you can bring that purpose to bear in your life.

6. It will give you insight into the most beneficial changes you can make and the options that lie before you.

7. It could even save your life. (Countless individuals claim

to have been saved by their intuition. Winston Churchill, for instance, said that listening to his intuition had kept him alive on a number of occasions, from his days in Africa through to the Second World War. In one of these instances, while visiting an anti-aircraft battery during a bombing raid, he sat in the staff car on the opposite side from where he would usually sit. During that drive, a bomb exploded so near the car that it was actually lifted into the air, but Churchill was saved. When his relieved wife asked him later that day why he had made that choice, he told her, 'Something said "Stop!" before I reached the car door held open for me. It then appeared to me that I was told I was meant to open the door on the other side and get in there – and that's what I did!'⁴)

BREAK THROUGH

Your intuitive self is taking you for a drive in a car. You are seated next to it. Close your eyes and 'take a look'. Where is it taking you? What colour is the car? How fast are you going? How comfortable do you feel letting your intuition drive in your life?

Besides creating clarity out of confusion and being able to make the best choices, there are even greater results to developing a conscious rapport with your intuitive mind. Looking inward for answers instead of outside yourself will always bring a greater discovery of your strength, confidence and freedom in life.

The more you listen to your intuition, the easier *all* of your decision-making becomes – building trust in yourself and in your own ideas. And this growing trust will allow you to become more self-reliant and confident in your truth. Ultimately, the answer to 'Why use intuition?' is the same as the answer to 'What is intuition?' And that answer is:

> *Your intuition is your truth;*
> *it is the voice of your spirit.*

If you listen to the voice of your truth, you will start to be more true to yourself, no matter what obstacles lie before you. And the more you live your truth, the more you will feel the freedom to follow your dreams!

Lessons in Breaking Through

How does breakthrough happen in your life? Sometimes change requires nothing less than a revolution. When the situation is dire or you've been painted into a corner, there may not be any action available except one of sweeping significance. Yet, as the ancient Oriental text, *The Book of Changes* (also called *The I Ching*) tells us, 'Revolutions are extremely grave matters. They should be undertaken only under stress of direct necessity, when there is no other way out.'[5] It further shows us in verse after verse that far greater change is likely to occur with numerous and consistent small steps than with revolution, as reflected in titles such as 'Preponderance of the Small', 'The Gentle, Penetrating Wind', 'The Taming Power of the Small'.

Think about your own history for a moment. With the exception of those situations where a revolution was required (divorce, quitting a job, a sudden move, etc.), the times when you experienced the most profound and prolonged changes inwardly and outwardly were probably fuelled by consistent and persevering small steps in the direction of your dreams. You couldn't become a concert pianist the first, tenth or even fiftieth time you sit down at a piano. But with small steps and constancy of thought and action, you can achieve anything.

Throughout the world, the major achievements in art, music, architecture and society have come about through the combined and repeated efforts of the individuals and the community. There were inevitably failures along the way – but perhaps they should not be considered failures because even mistakes can be helpful steps toward success.

There is only one aspect of your evolution (or what I call the discovery of your greatness) that *must* be unfailing, and that is your commitment to it! Plans may fizzle, strategies may back-fire, and there may be days when your determination will dwindle. Yet if you return the following day (and the next and the next) to the path of your discovery, you will inevitably and inescapably meet that greatness.

Your intuition is the tour guide on your journey of discovery. And regardless of where you feel your intuitive skills are now, with practice you can take them to a higher level of experience. (Just as they, not coincidentally, can take *you* to a higher level of experience!)

Many of the techniques in this book are designed to help you build a greater rapport with your spirit, who speaks to you through your intuition. Scattered throughout the text are a number of spontaneous exercises titled 'Break Through'. Most of these are extremely brief, requiring only a moment or two of your time; a few may take several minutes. They are designed to help you build your trust; spontaneity; powers of intuitive obser-vation; imaging skills; your trust; the awareness of your ever-present spirit; the habit of going inwards for your answers; a higher level of self-understanding and investigation; and, finally, did I mention trust?

No matter how much you may want to continue reading the text, when you come to a 'Break Through' take a moment to *do* the process. Let your ability to image and to imagine give you every idea, thought and picture – or even the tiniest fragment of an idea. *And trust everything you perceive!* There are no right or wrong answers. Whatever you notice is what's right for you.

These 'Break Through' exercises can become the lifeboats that take you away from the murky waters of confusion and into a greater understanding of yourself and your life. Like the 'unsinkable' Molly Brown, pick up the oars and take charge! Embrace everything that comes up for you without doubt or hesitation.

Break through to perceive what comes to mind. Determine what the image or concept means for you and how you feel about it. If you don't have a clue about what it means, just notice how you feel. If you can make a note about your perceptions in your journal or on a piece of paper, take a moment to do so. But if you don't have the time for that, don't let that keep you from doing the exercise. *The more you do these exercises, the more familiar you will become with spontaneously slipping in and out of your intuitive perspective!* You will quite literally experience a breakthrough each and every time you do an exercise.

Since these exercises are a very significant 'leg-up' onto the intuitive horse, be sure to do each 'Break Through' when you come to it (even when you open the book randomly or it falls open to one by accident). You can do any 'Break Through' exercise any number of times since the experience will be different in some way each time. Every time you experience a 'Break Through' you gain a little more insight into your self and your life; you heighten your ability to trust your spirit; you increase your comfort level with your intuitive voice; and you elevate the regard you hold for your intuition (which actually reflects the regard you hold for yourself).

In the *Book of Changes (The I Ching)*, the verse called 'Break-Through' is also called 'Resoluteness'. Be resolute in your commitment to these steps of development. If at first you don't feel you're getting anywhere, keep doing the exercises anyway. Even a substance as hard as granite will soften under the persistence of a tiny but ever constant drop of water! Your small steps will take you where you are meant to go. So be sure to break through, and break through, and then break through again. These are the steps in the discovery of your greatness.

Thus the superior man
of devoted character
Heaps up small things
In order to achieve something
high and great.[6]

– 'Pushing Upward',
The I Ching, verse 46

* * * * *

2

What's Your IQ (Intuition Quotient)?

Several factors (many of which may surprise you) indicate a strong disposition toward intuitive abilities. The IQ test below will help you assess where your inclinations are. Fear not, though, if you don't get a high score initially. The intuitive voice is as fundamental a component in every person's make-up as thought and emotion are. And with a little practice you can discover *your* spirit's voice and successfully employ a greater part of your intuitive awareness. So, read on and learn about your natural strengths and weaknesses (those points which will require more of your effort). Don't forget, self-discovery is what intuition is all about!

Test Your Intuition Quotient

Instructions: Choose a number between 1 and 10 for each answer (with a score of 10 for Always, 5 for Sometimes and 1 for Rarely). Be honest! When you've finished, check what your total score indicates. Then take a look at the 'Increase Your Intuition Quotient' section and begin your personal journey of intuitive development.

I: Your Intuition in Action

1. Have you ever had hunches about significant opportunities, situations or events before they occurred?

2. Have you ever had a troubling 'feeling' or physical discomfort when pursuing a choice that you *knew* wasn't in your best interest?

3. Have you ever had goose bumps, butterflies in the stomach, chills or other physical sensations, especially when having vague or undetermined feelings of anticipation?

4. Have you ever intentionally tuned in with your intuition in times of change, opportunity, confusion or ambivalence?

5. When you do experience your intuitive voice, do you try to be conscious of the different methods it uses to speak to you (images, ideas, gut feelings, physical sensations or emotions)?

6. Have you ever anticipated little daily occurrences before they happened (such as phone calls, e-mails, chance meetings, schedule changes, etc.)?

7. Are you ever able to sense others' feelings and concerns without having been informed of them directly?

8. Are you as willing to act upon the directions of your intuitive voice when it asks you to do something challenging as when it directs you towards something pleasurable and fun?

II: Your Intuitive Personality Profile
(Keep scoring 1 through 10 as in Part I of the test.)

1. Do you consider yourself creative and/or imaginative?

2. Do you feel that you are independent, confident and self-aware?

3. Are you open-minded, curious and eager to learn new things?

4. Do you consider yourself flexible, spontaneous and willing to change (both yourself and your schedule) or are you always in a hurry with your mind set on a fixed agenda?

5. Are you aware of your surroundings and sensitive to others around you?

6. Are you willing to take action in areas of your life that may be untested and untried?

7. Are you conscious of your body's needs and of its messages to you? Do you honour them? Are you also aware of the ebbs and flows of your energy patterns and what they mean?

8. Do you possess a willingness to know and grow, even when the pursuit of your growth may not necessarily take you down the easiest path?

9. Do you take your commitments seriously enough to embrace them with enthusiasm?

10. Do you live with integrity? In other words, are you honest with yourself and others in all matters, little and large?

Scoring Your IQ Test

121–180 points: Congratulations! If you reached this score, then you've had enough intuitive experiences to be familiar with that voice inside you. You also embrace the qualities that give you the strength to act on your intuition. If you continue to strive in making these personal qualities and intuitive practices real every day, then you will bring yourself ever closer to a greater realisation of success and happiness in your life (through both your intuitive guidance and your confident and joyful sense of self).

61–120 points: Falling into this score range means only one thing: you're pretty close to normal as far as your intuition and life's ups and downs have taken you. If you commit now to discovering the strength of your inner spirit, and to the activities and practices of listening to its voice, then you will be surprised at the new and abundant opportunities that can become available to you.

18–60 points: Don't worry! No matter what your score was, the situation is hardly hopeless. It may seem that your intuition has been eluding you all your life, but it's actually much more likely that *you* have been ignoring (or even suppressing) *it*! Still, there is work to be done, both in your intuitive exercises and in the discovery of your spirit. Fear not, though, with a little bit of effort, consistency in behaviour, and some changes in attitude, you will be able to discover the part of yourself which can take you to greatness!

Before continuing, briefly review your test to see which individual items need more of your attention. Read the next section for helpful suggestions about each item, staying mindful of the specific areas which may need improvement.

Increase Your Intuition Quotient

(a point-by-point consideration: Where to go from here)

This section allows you to read through each point and consider the steps that you can take to begin your programme of intuitive development. Be sure to pay special attention to your low-scoring test questions in order to determine the areas that may require special effort on your part.

I: Your Intuition in Action

1. Have you ever had hunches about significant opportunities, situations, or events before they occurred?
These hunches happen to everybody with varying degrees of strength and frequency. The plot of the award-winning film *Notorious* (starring Cary Grant and Ingrid Bergman) resulted from an initial hunch by the director, Alfred Hitchcock. He shared this hunch with his writer and it paid off. The story of secret uranium shipments proved to be not only wildly popular at the box office but also eerily prophetic, since the screenplay had been written (by Hitchcock's friend Ben Hecht) a full year before news of the atom bomb and the Manhattan Project came to light.[7]

Whether or not hunches are a part of your history, you can start to build a greater receptivity by staying more actively conscious of these spontaneous insights. Carry a small notebook with you and jot down a word or two whenever these hunches occur – even if the subject matter is about mundane tasks or seemingly unimportant events. By staying alert for these hunches in order to make a note of them, you will keep your intuitive radar sharp and become more sensitive to further feelings of expectancy.

2. Have you ever had a troubling 'feeling' or physical discomfort when pursuing a choice that you knew wasn't in your best interests?

Believe it or not, some feelings of discomfort – both emotional and physical – are good. They are the warning signals that you may not have honoured the voice of truth inside you. If you feel a pervasive discomfort in your daily life, then you have disregarded some important truth for too long and in too significant a way. Take a moment each night to consider in your journal any activity, relationship or behaviour about which you are uncomfortable. Think about why you made those choices, what you might have done differently, and what you need to do to feel a greater sense of well-being about this situation in the future.

3. Have you ever had goose bumps, butterflies in the stomach, chills or other physical sensations, especially when having vague or undetermined feelings of anticipation?

Although some of these physical sensations may be a little uncomfortable, they are not like the nagging discomfort discussed in question 2 (where you are troubled by the feeling of not having honoured yourself). These physical symptoms, on the other hand, are alerting you to take note of what's going through your mind and what's happening around you. Whether you're currently conscious of these physical reactions or not, try to become more aware of your body and the little sensations that move through it every day. When you recognise them, make a note about them in your journal, and about the deeper thoughts and/or circumstances occurring at those times.

4. Have you ever intentionally tuned in with your intuition in times of change, opportunity, confusion or ambivalence?
Even if this is not a habit that you have already cultivated, it is never too late to start. Before making important decisions, or when you have several options to consider, take a few moments to quiet your mind and ask for an image. It doesn't have to be *an answer*, just an idea, an image or a symbol. You don't even have to know what it means. Just close your eyes and ask your inner guidance for a simple thought, concept, or even 'picture'. Notice what you immediately perceive and put it in your notebook. Wait a day (or at least several hours) and ask again. Don't analyse, just be receptive. See what images are brought to you. Notice how you feel about them and about the possibilities that lie before you.

5. When you do experience your intuitive voice, do you try to be conscious of the different methods it uses to speak to you (images, ideas, gut feelings, physical sensations or emotions)?
This is perhaps the easiest practice to pursue in your daily life. If you're already staying alert for your intuitive moments, all you have to do is notice *how* they happen as well. Some people may be more 'visual', others more 'verbal', and still others more 'sentient' (knowing or sensing). Becoming familiar with your own intuitive process helps you to know where you are most open to your own intuitive symbols.

6. Have you ever anticipated little daily occurrences before they happened (such as phone calls, e-mails, chance meetings, schedule changes, etc.)?
I have a friend who always wakes up two minutes before her alarm rings (perhaps in order to avoid the 'alarm' to her system). Another friend can always tell what time it is and knows who's calling on her cell phone (though not on her home phone) before she answers it.

If you haven't noticed such a facility with these minor every-day events yet, it is very easy to initiate this practice. Before you leave the house in the morning, just close your eyes and 'look' for the faces that you're going to see that day. If you're not particularly accurate when playing these little games of intuition, don't despair. The important intuitive messages (those with strong emotional content and greater life significance) are usually easier to read because they are more powerful and penetrating in your experience. As we will see in Chapter 12, these types of exercises are very much like scales for a pianist: they keep the muscles flexed, but will rarely be as important (both in execution and in the experience) as the symphony.

7. Are you ever able to sense others' feelings and concerns without having been informed of them directly?

Emotional sensitivity is only one step removed from intuitive sensitivity, and in many ways the two are connected. Open yourself to sensing what others around you may be feeling – at the office, at home, even in the supermarket or on the bus. You don't have to give this (or any of these practices) a lot of your time. Just moments will do. Simply 'touch in', acknowledge what you perceive, and release. And don't worry about 'catching' others' feelings. You don't have to drown (or even swim) in other people's emotional pools to sense the feelings that are washing over them. Just take a moment to tune in, notice what you feel (and *how* you feel), and then tune out.

8. Are you as willing to act upon the directions of your intuitive voice when it asks you to do something challenging as when it directs you toward something pleasurable and fun?

We must embrace our lives with joy and with purpose. Each is as important as the other, and sometimes neither comes easy. Often, though, we choose only what is easiest. And, as the saying goes, the path of least resistance rarely leads to the remarkable.

Make a commitment to choose at least one little thing each day that your intuitive voice tells you to do in order to create greater joy in your heart. If these directives require broad-sweeping change or extensive action, determine one small step you can take – every day!

II: Your Intuitive Personality Profile

While the qualities discussed in Part II of the test may not *seem* to have anything to do with being intuitive, they are as important as any technical skill you can develop (for they are the attributes that allow you to be truly guided by your inner voice). In the end, the biggest difference between non-intuitive people and those who are highly developed is not how much they *perceive* their intuition, but how much they *act* upon it. After all, anyone with enough determination can be taught a skill, but how easy is it to teach someone determination?

> *Ultimately, those who won't listen to their intuition are much worse off than those who can't – because those who can't can learn!*

Using the following point-by-point approach, consider the new perspectives, attitudes, and strengths that you can pursue to improve your intuitive abilities (as well as your life).

1. Do you consider yourself creative and/or imaginative?

People who are creative (who can 'think outside the box') tend not to limit themselves exclusively to analytical thought. Over-analysis of any information, especially intuitive information, can inhibit your ability to take action. Like Shakespeare's tragic hero, Hamlet, one of the best ways *not to do* something is to keep thinking about it! If you tend to over-analyse the decisions in your life, try to become more aware of this habit as it's happening. Throughout your day practise making decisions on minor matters more spontaneously and intuitively; determine what you *feel* in your gut (not only what you *think*) and then act upon it.

Intuitive messages often take the form of ideas or *images* that suddenly pop into the mind through the *image*-ination. If you're already imaginative, your ability to recognise those images will strongly support your intuitive experiences. Don't worry, though, if you didn't score highly on this one. We'll look at some exercises later to 'tweak' your imaging skills.

2. Do you feel that you are independent, confident and self-aware?

Being independent is not the same as being a loner, being aggressive or being selfish. It simply means that you trust yourself enough to know what's best for you and that you have the courage to see it through. Scoring well on this question indicates that you probably won't be intimidated when choosing what your intuitive voice tells you to do – even when those choices may be challenged by well-meaning others.

If your score for this question was low, begin now to *believe* that you have a powerful truth inside you. Find some affirmations that you can repeat every day to help you redefine yourself in your spirit. Affirmations are simple sentences which help you focus your intention. They can replace old, negative belief systems with new, powerful truths, such as 'I am blessed with the ability to live my dreams.' Begin to believe in that self and in that spirit. The more confident and self-accepting you are, the more willing you will be to listen to your own inner guidance. And, not coincidentally, the more you listen inside, the more confident you will become. (For more affirmations, see Appendix A.)

3. Are you open-minded, curious and eager to learn new things?
The very nature of intuition requires you to perceive information that doesn't come to you through your physical senses. You must open your mind to accept a concept of reality that is larger than the physical self and perhaps even larger than space or time. If you are already open-minded, be sure to maintain a strong curiosity about things that may be unseen and perhaps even unseeable. Always seek to discover new worlds wherever you go.

4. Do you consider yourself flexible, spontaneous and willing to change (both yourself and your schedule) or are you always in a hurry with your mind set on a fixed agenda?
In her stand-up comedy act, Rita Rudner declares, 'I never panic when I get lost. I just change where I want to go!' While this may be a little too spontaneous (it is a joke after all), it's good to be flexible in your life.

Spontaneous intuition happens when it happens. If you are stuck in a rut with your eyes set only on a predetermined agenda, you will not be free to step upon new paths of opportunity. You will miss messages from your spirit which could have the potential to guide you to greatness. You may certainly succeed in checking off every single item on your list of things to do, but will you also check in with every unplanned opportunity as well? To increase your flexibility, change your days a little and stay conscious of how you meet with obstructions in your schedule. Instead of becoming angry, just ask yourself, 'What or whom am I supposed to find on this detour?' If you look for the benefit, you *will* find it – even if it's simply a few extra minutes to catch your breath and centre yourself while waiting in a long queue. Always assume that there is a purpose in every little event and seek to discover it! This increases your spontaneity and your awareness of synchronicity (the seemingly coincidental timing of events, which will be discussed later).

5. Are you aware of your surroundings and sensitive to others around you?

Building sensitivity to your environment and to the people within it is a large step forward in your intuitive development. It is a good idea to practise opening your sensitivity to people and places as a conscious activity on a regular basis. So, try this exercise several times a week. When you walk into a room, look around for a moment and ask yourself what you 'sense' about the people there or about the room itself. Remember, you are trying to discern what you feel, not only what you observe. It's not necessary to analyse or draw conclusions. Just notice what you feel, and then go on about your day. Doing this exercise frequently will help you build the habit of looking for information that isn't immediately apparent through observation alone, information that comes from your intuitive voice.

6. Are you willing to take action in areas of your life that may be untested and untried?

Having the courage to go somewhere you've never been before is essential in learning to work with your intuition – first, in trusting your intuitive experiences and, second, in having the strength to pursue a challenging new direction which may be guided by your inner voice. This does not refer to how fearless you are. We are all afraid at some time in our lives. This courage is more about how willing you are to confront your fears, especially when pursuing a compelling course of action which may not have a foreseeable result. So, don't be afraid to listen to the voice of your spirit, and don't be afraid to get to know your fears. Meet your fears, and you will discover that they could well be the maps to your life's destinations.

7. Are you conscious of your body's needs and of its messages to you? Do you honour them? Are you also aware of the ebbs and flows of your energy patterns and what they mean?

Your body talks to you all the time, giving you messages about all areas of your life – physical, mental, emotional and intuitive. When you are listening to the voice of your spirit, you wake up with enthusiasm, vitality and the energy to pursue your dreams. When you block your inner guidance, you will find your energy blocked and faltering. Your body can give you headaches when you have too many worries on your mind. It can give you indigestion when you eat foods that aren't good for it. And when you're depressed, your immune system can get depressed, too, leaving you fatigued and more susceptible to colds and flu. Your body can give you specific intuitive messages as well. (One author and famously successful investor, George Soros, could tell that there was something wrong with his portfolio when he got a backache!) Yet many people ignore most messages from their bodies, putting their physical needs far below career, family and even household errands. When your body wants to provide an intuitive insight, how prepared do you think you will be if you are not even in the habit of listening to it for its most obvious requests of rest, good food and exercise? Begin now to notice what your body is telling you. If you're not sure of the message, close your eyes and ask it. You don't need to be able to interpret every sign right away. Just give yourself a chance to consciously connect with this most valuable source of information, energy and life.

8. Do you possess a willingness to know and grow, even when the pursuit of your growth may not necessarily take you down the easiest path?

When you make listening a habit and do what your intuitive voice tells you – what your *truth* tells you – you will discover a greater happiness and your life will be filled with an unshakeable

sense of well-being. But this happiness does not always translate as 'easiness'. There will definitely be times when what you
'hear' from your intuition will not be what you want to hear. It
may be something as drastic as the need to leave a toxic relationship or as basic as the need to read a certain book or cut fats
out of your diet. Regardless of the message or its ease, if it rings
true and you *don't* pursue it, you will find your life wanting.

There have already been many truthful perceptions in your
life that you have chosen to ignore or do little about just because
it's easier that way. But staying on 'easy street' really only keeps
you stuck between a rock and a hard place.

> *If you want to be able to know your truth*
> *(or hear your intuitive voice), you must be*
> *willing to know your truth and stop living in*
> *denial. And you must then be willing to act*
> *upon your truth as well.*

To pursue actively the voice of your spirit, you must be honest
with yourself and look for your truth in everything, whether or
not it leads you down the path of least resistance. To practise
this, take at least one small step each day in a challenging action
which you have been avoiding, an action that honours your commitment to your truth. With each passing day take another step
forward and then another. Before you know it, you'll be happy to
leave 'the big easy' for a place called joy.

9. Do you take your commitments seriously enough to embrace them with enthusiasm?

Though having commitments may seem to contradict the qualities of flexibility and spontaneity (as discussed in question four)
it only *seems* that way. Being spontaneous and flexible doesn't
mean that you live life without commitments. Indeed, when you

commit yourself to listening to your intuition, you are actually making a commitment to staying flexible. Flexibility and spontaneity are absolutely necessary if you are going to be free to act upon the directives of your intuition. Sometimes those directives may cause a logistical challenge in keeping other commitments. For instance, you may be a devoted single mother who is inwardly being guided to take an art class which is offered only when your kids are at home. If you enthusiastically embrace both commitments, you will happily *seek and discover* options that will satisfy both commitments (baby-sitters, alternative classes, etc.).

When you hold your commitments solely out of obligation and duty, you will no longer feel that you have a sense of choice. And without choice, the only activities you'll pursue will be the most urgent ones or those that make you feel the most guilty. Doing what your inner voice tells you to do will become a distant dream, and every obligation you meet will be filled with resistance and resentment.

If you feel that your present commitments drag you down and depress you, there are some changes you can make. First and foremost, see your choice in everything. When you don't recognise that you have a choice in every action, you abdicate your power to make your own choices in the future. You abdicate the power to take action on your own behalf.

> *Determine what you can do to create*
> *a more balanced integration between*
> *your choices for others and*
> *your choices for yourself.*

Once you recognise that you always have options, consider what you need to do to exercise those options in the best way possible for all concerned. Redesign those commitments that you find obstructive in terms of scheduling and logistics. Most importantly, re-evaluate those commitments that bring you the greatest emotional strife, those which conflict with your commitment to your well-being and to your joy. (See Chapter 6 for more on the commitment conundrum.)

10. Do you live with integrity? In other words, are you honest with yourself and others in all matters, little and large?

Do you choose actions that are absolutely right for you? It's important to understand that what *you* determine to be right or wrong has nothing to do with what others say is right or wrong. A certain action may even be 'right' at one time and not the next, but it is still you who must decide.

During a very trying time in Mahatma Gandhi's life, when his politics sparked many volatile situations, twice in one day he found himself in the midst of dangerous crowds. On the first occasion he confronted the crowds; on the second, he slipped away to safety by disguising himself. He was confused about the two opposite actions being 'true' for him. 'Who can say for certain that I was right both when I faced the crowd in the first instant bravely, as it was said, and when I escaped from it in disguise? ...judging a man from his outward act is no more than a doubtful inference.'[8]

Though he had been kicked and pelted with stones in the first incident, his wounds were not severe. When the police asked Gandhi if he wanted to prosecute his assailants he said that since he was unable to judge his own disparate actions, he could not judge others. On each occasion his only choice had been to do what was right in his heart – to live with his truth at that very moment.

In order to make your intuitive voice a priority, you must first hold your integrity in high regard and seek your truth in all that you do.

*Knowing your spirit and living in falsehood
cannot simultaneously co-exist.*

If you find yourself making choices that *feel* wrong (and ultimately hurtful) in relationships and behaviour, then you have
already created a certain comfort level with falsehood. Never
make it easy for you to *lie to yourself*. Instead, seek your truth,
know your truth, and *live* your truth in everything and with
everyone!

* * * * *

3

Spontaneous Intuition:
Waking to the Whispers

Practically everyone has had an intuitive occurrence at some time or other – even those who would put it down to 'chance' have had some sort of prescient experience. Perhaps you've had the urge to drive down a certain lane in a full car park and suddenly someone pulls out just in time to let you have the space, or maybe you've known when a loved one needed a call. Now, if you don't believe in intuition, you might call such a happening a lucky coincidence. Yet, whatever you call it, it is still a textbook case of intuition – the act of knowing something without the use of physical senses or conscious reasoning.

The intuitive voice speaks much more frequently than most of us realise. Unfortunately, we often choose to disregard this voice. Some people do so because they feel that it can't be valid, not having a rational or 'knowable' source. Others are simply *too busy* to let intuitive impressions sneak in among the numerous other thoughts that are part of the daily business of living. And still others ignore the subtle messages of intuition because they need to be hit over the head with a 'sign' before they will believe. (Lightning bolts or manna from heaven may not even do it for some!)

The worst reason of all for not listening to our intuition is that we don't value ourselves enough to believe that important

information can come from within. Unlike all other species in
the world, we humans are the only animals willing (indeed,
needing) to trust another's opinion before our own instincts.
When we have important decisions to make, we may get two or
three professional opinions and poll all our friends before we
listen to ourselves. Yet life-changing decisions require the most
attentive inner listening and absolute trust in everything we
hear. Listening is the first step in spontaneous intuition and the
first step in living your truth.

Spontaneous Intuition: Four Simple Steps

1. Listen
2. Trust
3. Respond
4. Investigate

Step 1:
Make Listening a Habit

The first task in developing your intuitive experience is a simple
one: practise listening. Your intuition is always present, even
when you're not focusing on it. Begin to make a mindful effort
to notice when this still, small voice speaks within you. You may
think that you don't know what this voice sounds like, but in
fact it's more a question of what it *feels* like. (Intuitive information can come in words, ideas and images, but mostly in
feelings.) Your intuition has been directing you with varying
degrees of success all of your life. You will usually recognise this
voice not by the sound it makes or by the specifics of the message, but by the sense of being compelled by it. A thought will
capture your attention (or a feeling will grab your gut) and won't
let go. All you have to do now is stay more conscious of when
you sense this feeling inside you. When you do, stop for a
moment and notice what it's trying to tell you. If you can't under-

stand the message exactly, just observe what you feel, how you feel, and what you perceive.

It's important to note that practising spontaneous intuition is rather like practising sneezing. The practice part obviously alters the spontaneous part. There are many specific techniques for developing *applied* intuition (which we'll look into later), but for now the best way to start is to learn how to become more comfortable with your spontaneous intuitive voice.

Listening may not be as simple as it seems. Our thought processes are very undisciplined and our minds are often filled with scattered ideas. The intuitive voice must push through this wall of clutter just to be heard. Often this mental clutter is one of the main reasons that our experience of intuition is so fleeting and ill-defined. We perceive just a little corner of a picture or part of an idea, before it is pushed away by other thoughts and feelings. (We will discuss these other internal voices throughout Part II. For now, the first step is simply to direct your listening inwards.)

In order to practise listening, it's necessary to practise quieting the mind. Take a few minutes now to give the next exercise a try and take your first step into conscious listening.

READY, SET, GO!
Learning to Listen

PURPOSE: To quieten the mind and clear it of mental clutter so that your intuition can have a larger voice in your life. (Please note that there are no expectations attached to this process. You cannot be 'right' or 'wrong'. This is merely a simple practice in observing and stilling the mind.)

PREPARATION: If you choose to maintain this process for more than ten minutes, it would be best if you turn off your phones and other sources of distraction and find a room in which you will not be interrupted. You could also do this process for just a few minutes at a time as you go about your day.

STEPS:

1. Sit in a comfortable position. Close your eyes and take a deep, relaxing breath. Allow yourself to continue to relax as your breathing becomes more steady and easy.

2. Bring your consciousness away from the myriad thoughts and ideas tumbling around in your head and begin to look for the quiet. Begin to *listen* to the quiet.

3. If it seems difficult to listen to stillness, begin instead to listen to the sound of your breath. Hold a restful word in your mind – peace, harmony, love or gentleness – and think about it with each inhalation.

4. If distracting thoughts pop up in your mind, acknowledge them briefly and let them go. Then turn your mind and your heart back to your breath and to the idea of peace.

5. Hold this focus for at least a few minutes. If you do this several times a day, you will be able to train your mind to turn away from clutter and noise and turn towards that peaceful place within you where your intuition resides.

OBSERVATION: The mind is always busy and active, so bringing stillness to all of this chaos takes practice. That's why listening to your breath and holding a peaceful mental focus will help to keep other thoughts from filling your consciousness. Doing this will also help you respond to your day in a calmer, more balanced way. While you're listening to your breathing, try not to think about particular problems or look for any answers. Simply look for the stillness, the stillness that goes with the state of listening.

THE NEXT STEP: After you have practised this process with your eyes closed, try it briefly with your eyes open, maintaining the focus of your breathing without letting the visual activity around you distract you. Do this for just a moment here and a few minutes there. If you practise quieting the chaotic mind and learn to listen to nothing, the 'nothing' you hear will ultimately open the door to the voice of everything!

*　　*　　*　　*　　*

Step 2:
Trust Everything You Perceive

Trust is the most important key in working with your intuition, in listening to your spirit, in appreciating your self, in living your life. In the end, it may be the only key. You may have a natural talent for intuitive perception, but if you are not able to trust what you experience, the information you perceive will not get you very far. If you are always silencing your inner voice with doubts and second guesses, then even the finger of God could point the way and you would deny yourself the trip!

Trust is the first and last word in the lexicon of your spirit. Yet trust is much more than a word and more than a frame of mind. It is an action. Trust is the action taken by your consciousness when it does *not* dismiss an idea or a gut feeling just because there was no physical stimulus for it, or – even worse – just because it came from you. Isn't it odd that we are often so quick to seek the advice of others yet are so easily dismissive of our own ideas and abilities, even of our value?

BREAK THROUGH

You are standing on a ledge about as high up as you are tall. The jump down isn't dangerous, but it is a little daunting. You'd feel much better if you knew someone would be there to break your fall. And, suddenly, there is! You look down from your perch and discover that the person there to catch you is you! How do you feel? Do you hesitate or falter even for a moment, or do you jump?

In the personal and temporal world, our value is all too often assessed in terms of comparison to others, never as an absolute. This is an unnatural state for our spirit, who tells us that the state of perfection is complete and eternally enduring. Since we are *both* spirit and human (for the time being, anyway), we have the opportunity to choose which definition to believe. Right now, and at any moment in your life, you can choose either to see yourself as lacking or to recognise your complete potential in any endeavour. Which would you rather believe about yourself? Which belief would help you trust yourself more? Indeed, which belief is your highest truth?

A friend once told me a story of her husband's intuitive feeling at an airport – not necessarily the easiest place to start working with intuition. While they were waiting for her to board the plane for a business trip, he started to become uneasy. Although he knew it was a very important trip, he asked her not to go. He became so agitated that finally he began to cry. Ultimately, she was able to ease his fears, but she did not change her travel plans. As it turned out, the hydraulics on the aircraft failed *before* they could taxi down the runway. Fortunately, she and the other passengers were then safely put on another plane. It's important to notice, though, that it was not her husband's intuition that failed. What was found wanting was his wife's ability to *trust* his intuitive experience.

The action of trust begins with believing – or at least seriously considering – your intuitive perceptions. But belief is only the beginning. You must then act on that trust; you must respond!

Step 3:
Respond to Your Intuitive Voice

After you recognise and believe your intuitive voice, the next step is to respond to the information you are given. In other words, *do what you are told!*

Of course, this does not mean that you should make it a habit to act precipitously – just, perhaps, a little bit more spontaneously. In significant matters, certainly, it is always necessary to consider all of the important factors – and *then* do what your intuition tells you. You will never be steered in the wrong direction by your own spirit. As a matter of fact, if you discover that you have taken a wrong turn in your life, you may find that you have been listening to your worries, your guilt, your ego or your lower emotions. All of these are important voices to hear because they, too, have something to show you about your truth, but they should not necessarily direct your actions or decisions. (We'll take a look at these other important voices in the next section.)

The practice of doing what your intuition tells you to do may require you to be a little more flexible in both the minor and major activities of your day. I am not suggesting that if you get the need to take a walk in the park, you should just forget about work or any other commitments you might have. On the other hand, if you have a *compelling feeling* that you must go to the park at a certain time, then you may want to reshape your day (if it's possible) so that you can do that and still fulfil your other obligations.

BREAK THROUGH

It's time to check your calendar for tomorrow's list of things to do. On it you see that your intuitive self has added one further item. Close your eyes. What is it? Will you make time to do it?

Of course, much of what you receive through spontaneous intuition will be about relatively small matters that occur throughout the day. Yet sometimes these seemingly minor matters – such as turning left instead of right, calling a certain person on the phone, buying a particular book even if you don't really know why you want it – can have more important consequences later.

Though my brother-in-law, Benjamin, had had a dream about a car accident a few nights in a row, he hadn't given it much credence. He hadn't been worried about his own car because it was running well and had been regularly serviced. Then one day a month later as he was driving to work, he got a strong compulsion to have the car serviced, even though it wasn't yet time. The next day he had the same feeling again, along with a fleeting idea (actually an image) of a telephone pole right in front of him. This time he knew it was his intuition talking. He took the car to his mechanic that same day. When they examined it, they discovered a tie rod hanging on by a thread. Just one more day of deliberating could have been one day too many.

Sometimes, the most important action you can ever take is to trust your intuition.

Had Benjamin not listened to his intuition, the telephone pole might have ended up through his windscreen. The image could also have represented an urgent 'call' from his spirit. Regardless, Benjamin took action!

Not all bits of intuitive information are this significant. Usually they are simply about the minor events that take place every day. Yet, even these are very important to act upon when listening to the intuitive voice.

I recall an incident late one night when I kept *feeling* that I needed to turn out the garage light, in spite of the fact that I clearly remembered having done so. That memory was so strong that I spent an hour telling my intuition that it was crazy (which was a waste of energy, considering it would have taken me about thirty seconds to go to the garage and check). In spite of my stubbornness when I'm 'sure' I'm right, my intuitive feeling was relentless, and I finally submitted to it. When I opened the door to the garage I discovered that the light was indeed already off *and* that my cat had been mistakenly locked inside. Although this situation was certainly not life-altering, my cat was happy with the result and so was I (since there's no litter tray in the garage!).

In this event, my original perception was not correct, but my *responsive action* – go to the garage – certainly was. (For some reason, this is a common occurrence when working with intuition.) This situation illustrates how important responding is.

Yet, even if there had been no result whatsoever, it still would have been important to react – simply because *the act of responding builds the practice of responding.* Taking the action to respond is necessary to complete the intuitive process.

> *In the end, no matter how well you listen to your intuition, if you don't respond it will never make a difference in your life.*

Why on earth, though, would we consider any one of these unimportant events (a light left on all night, a cat stuck in a garage) worthy of a second thought, let alone worthy of our time and effort in using them to practise intuitive development? And even if the intuitive feelings are accurate, how can such trivial matters increase our lives in any significant way?

First of all, you never can tell when a monumental – possibly life-changing – opportunity may turn on a tiny, seemingly meaningless event. (I have a client in New York City who met her next boss because a friend was late for a meeting.) Secondly, and most importantly, it is the daily, little-event type of listening that creates the everyday relationship with the voice of your spirit. Only through consistent exposure to the smaller and *regular* experiences of your intuition, does this inner wisdom become more accessible in the larger decisions and actions of your life.

After all, when you first learned to read, you didn't start with *War and Peace*. To learn the language of your intuitive mind and know your spirit's voice, you must first start with the little words or the mundane (and frequent) daily messages. After you have begun to trust and respond to these little (and sometimes larger) messages, it is then time to investigate.

Step 4:

Investigate the Results

Once you have taken the action requested by your intuitive voice, it's important to investigate the results of that action. Sometimes the benefit resulting from your instincts is immediately apparent. You might discover that the left turn you took helped you to avoid a traffic jam. Or the friend you felt you just had to call was in need of your support in some way. At other times you may not know for a while whether your instincts led you to the right course of action. That certain book you felt you had to buy may sit on your shelf for weeks until the moment your son or daughter needs it in the middle of the night for a late assignment.

Sometimes the benefits of listening to your intuition may not make themselves known for years or, indeed, they may be so subtle in nature that they don't seem apparent. Sometimes we may feel that we're being led down the wrong path at first, but later we may discover that in spite of a false start or difficulties encountered, it was the best way after all.

On a particular day during the Second World War, my father had a strong impulse to seek cover away from the rest of his squad while they were under enemy fire. Because of this impulse he was the only man injured that day. I'm sure he thought at the time that his intuition had misdirected him until one day several weeks later. While he was recovering from that injury in an army hospital well away from the front, his entire squad was killed by snipers.

Investigating the results of listening to your intuition – although those results may not always be apparent – can be helpful in many ways:

- *It confirms your accurate responses* and therefore reinforces your commitment to continue listening to your intuition.

- *It helps you to become familiar with your intuitive voice* through observation – making it easier with time to distinguish it from the other voices that speak within you (such as your emotions).

- *It allows you consciously to link the actions you take to the intuition that directs them.* Thus, you begin to form the habit of looking to your intuitive mind for direction *before* you take action and make important decisions. (This is a significant step which will ultimately take you from spontaneous intuition to applied intuition.)

- *It enables you to build a stronger experience of trust and of belief in yourself, particularly when you pay attention to an intuitively directed action for which you see no immediate results.* Since the experience of intuition is entirely subjective and not available through the five physical senses, trust of and belief in the *inner* voice are absolutely required. *Determining that the subtle nuances of intuition are credible even when there are no apparent results is the highest form of trust you can create.*

- *It gives you the opportunity to define yourself from a higher perspective and to release your need to control the world outside yourself.* This leads to a new kind of trust – the belief that God and the part of yourself that is eternal and divine have a better vision of where you need to go and what you need to do, even though you may not understand why. Trust is also the faith that their voices work through you and speak to you, even if you don't know how. It is the foundation upon which all perception of spirit and of the higher mind is built.

A helpful technique when investigating the outcome of your intuitive responses is to practise looking for the inside meaning of the outer experiences in your life. Do this with the little events in your day, even when they don't seem to be directed by your intuition. For example, if you're late for a meeting and are stuck in a traffic jam, take a few moments to look for the 'reasons' (besides the broken water main that's flooding the intersection) why you might be there.

As you're sitting there and your blood begins to boil, remind yourself what a great opportunity to experience patience this is! Then take a deep breath and fill yourself with patience. And if you become worried about whether the person you're meeting will be angry or understanding, recall the times when you were not so understanding yourself. Then plant the suggestion in your mind to be more charitable in the future. And, oh, maybe the CD you've been looking for is in the glove box. And look! There's a wildflower garden over there! Isn't it beautiful? (As you can see, there can be many meanings behind even the smallest event.)

This practice can help you in many ways. First, looking for the meanings behind things helps you learn to investigate regularly the outcome of your intuition. And second, you will also discover a deeper appreciation of how 'coincidence' works in your world. (Psychologist Carl Jung preferred the term 'synchronicity', a much more precise description.)

> *Your intuition and your ability to recognise synchronicity are vitally important as you seek to know the hand of your spirit within your life.*

Of course, as Freud put it, sometimes a cigar is just a cigar! And you may find yourself in a totally mundane situation directed merely by the practicalities of life. But guess what? With the daily practice of looking for the larger meanings inside any outer experience, you might just discover heaven – at the dry cleaners!

Increasing Spontaneous Intuition

Writing Down the Bits and Pieces

One of the best ways to build up greater momentum in all four steps of developing your intuition is to start keeping a journal. It doesn't have to be a long or tedious task. Just note the bare bones of your intuitive experiences as they occur throughout your day. Often you will perceive only little bits or fragments, like pieces of a puzzle for which you don't have a complete picture. These little bits are very important to note in your journal because more fragments and a fuller picture are likely to appear over time. If you think you don't have time to keep a journal, consider Leonardo da Vinci, who wrote more than 14,000 journal pages – in backwards writing that could only be read in a mirror! (And this was in his spare time – between painting, sculpting, playing music, inventing, and buying caged birds in the street markets just so he could set them free!)

Writing about each intuitive feeling, your physical sensations, the images or ideas you had (and what you thought they meant), the action you took in responding to them, and the results of those actions can be of considerable help in developing your powers of observation and self-awareness. In this way you create the habit of looking for and identifying your intuition. Journal writing helps you build the practice of deliberating about your actions and seeking the involvement of your intuitive mind, the mind of your spirit. It also helps you to get to know yourself better. After all, the more practice you have in staying alert for your intuitive voice, the greater consideration you can give to all of the many voices within you and the messages that they offer. (Writing backwards is optional!)

R E A D Y ,   S E T ,   G O !
Creating an Intuition Journal

PURPOSE: To foster your powers of observation and keep your
   intuitive insights organised for future reference. Remember,
   sometimes the results of acting on your intuition require time to
   evolve – your journal will help you to keep track of your intuitive
   events over time.

PREPARATION: It would be most beneficial to carry a small pocket
   notebook with you throughout your day. This allows you to jot
   down just a word or two as your intuitive perceptions occur. If
   your time is restricted, you may wish to complete your journal
   entry later in the evening or before bed. This will give you an
   opportunity to review the day's events and the context in which
   your intuitive messages were received.

STEPS:

1. As the opportunity arises, make a simple note of any intuitive
   perceptions. You don't have to be sure it's your intuition. Simply
   note even an undefined feeling of anticipation or a fleeting
   fragment of an image or an idea. Also write about any directives
   or guidance that your insight may give you.

2. Keep it simple. You don't want this exercise to become too time-
   consuming. (If it does, you won't stay with it.) After you've noted
   your intuitive message, add a few words about the action you
   were able to take (or plan to take) to respond to it.

3. Also, notice the times when certain ideas or experiences resulted
   in a physical reaction on your part – goose bumps, chills, even a
   simple catch in your breath. If there's time, write about the
   thoughts and impressions that went through your mind when
   they occurred. If not, just jot down a few words that will trigger
   your memory and help you recall the incident later.

4. The voice of your intuition is often very soft and subtle, especially
   when you're just beginning. If you're not exactly sure if something
   was an intuitive experience, sit down at the end of your day and

write about the events that *seemed* like coincidences. That is often the best clue. *If you think it's a coincidence, it isn't.*

OBSERVATION: Sometimes it is not possible to act immediately on the advice of your intuition. Other times you may be able to take immediate action, but won't know the results of that action for months (submitting a business proposal that must be approved by many committees, for example). Right now new opportunities could be evolving in your life because of an intuitive direction you took long ago. For this reason, it's important to take a look back in your journal every now and again just to see what insights you've had in the past and where they've taken you. Don't discount the messages that did not *seem* to direct you to the right place. Your life isn't over yet, and the path determined by your intuition may have several strange twists and turns along the way.

THE NEXT STEP: As you become more accustomed to writing spontaneously about your intuitive experiences in your journal, you will begin to notice intuitive moments more frequently. At times you will also perceive brief images or fleeting ideas that may not seem complete or are perhaps quite obscure or meaningless.

Your intuitive mind speaks in symbols as well as in 'sensing' or gut feelings. We'll take a greater look at these symbols in Part III, but for now it's important to note the impressions you perceive regardless of whether or not you can interpret them clearly. Observation is an important step in applied intuition. So even if a symbol, image or idea seems enigmatic or even silly, just make a brief note of it in your journal. It will have more meaning for you later as you build a more conscious dialogue with your inner voice.

* * * * *

Personal Study for Part I

Use your journal to respond to the following questions.

1. You achieve what you believe, so begin now to change any limiting beliefs. On small index cards write a few sentences (affirmations) that reinforce your experience of your spirit, the voice of your intuition. Keep each statement simple with one affirmation to a card – for example, 'I discover a deeper power inside me every day' (see Appendix A for others). Think, too, of the unlimited benefit that listening to your spirit will bring. Write an affirmation answering 'What would I create if I could not fail?' Say these affirmations aloud to yourself in the mirror. Carry a few cards with you, and read them several times throughout your day.

2. In your journal or on a separate piece of paper, list some of the responses that you notice in your body and emotions during the listening exercise on page 33. Practise this exercise for five to ten minutes each day. It is the precursor to developing the techniques of applied intuition.

3. Take a moment or two to recall the past few days and think of any incident, no matter how small, when your intuition 'spoke' to you. (If you cannot recall any incidents, this is a good reason to start carrying a journal!) Write a few words about what form the message took, how you reacted, and whether or not you were able to investigate the outcome. Do this in your journal daily to help build the practice of trust.

4. Think of the time when your most recent coincidence occurred. Write down the possible meanings behind the outer experience, as shown in Investigate the Results. Also, practise this in your mind whenever the opportunity arises throughout your day, and then note your observations later in your journal.

Part II

Identifying the Voices
That Speak Within You

But ceremony never did conceal ...
How much we are the woods we wander in.

— Richard Wilbur

4

The Crowd and the Chorus

Become Conscious of the Chorus

As we have seen, trust is the keystone in all intuitive experiences, but you cannot trust what you are unable to perceive. The first step in building your skills of observation and staying alert for your intuitive voice is to give greater consideration to all of the many voices within you and to the messages they bring.

It is not at all an odd occurrence to have conversations going on inside your head. Most of us are engaged in back-and-forth thinking for much of our waking hours. You can 'hear' the various voices inside you discussing feelings and trying to make decisions. The voice of your emotions may argue with the voice of your reason when deciding whether to buy the nicer house or the one that fits your budget. And the voice of your body may challenge the voice of your conscience when you have to wake up at five in the morning on your day off to take the kids on a promised camping trip.

Considering how much time we spend talking to ourselves, it's amazing that we don't know ourselves better!

Before you can know the intuitive mind (the voice of your spirit) in your life, you have to learn to distinguish it from the many other voices within you – your fantasies, fears, hopes, worries – that talk to you all day. These can fill your waking hours like water trying to find its own level, seeping into the cracks and crevices of your mind even when you are trying to concentrate on work, fun, or simply on conversations with others.

Yet all this mental activity doesn't mean that your life has to become a playground for every random thought that wishes to bounce around your consciousness whenever and wherever it wants. Knowing your intuition requires knowing yourself. And knowing yourself means identifying the *source* of those internal voices that seek your attention throughout your day.

BREAK THROUGH

Close your eyes and notice all of the voices that make up the chorus inside you – your body, your ego, your emotions, your spirit, and even your analytical mind. Imagine them singing all at one time. Take a moment to notice this chorus within you. Even if you don't 'hear' this performance, how does it feel? Is it in sync? Or do the voices seem to be fighting each other? Which voice is the soprano (high) and which is the bass (low)? Which voice is the most off-key? And who is the conductor?

First, there is the voice of the body. Then there is the voice of your ego, your emotions, your conscience and, finally, your spirit (your soul, your higher mind or your intuition – whichever you prefer to call it). I don't pretend that these categories furnish a complete and comprehensive analysis of the psyche. As a matter of fact, your life and choices can be influenced by many *unknown* factors, such as unconscious habits, forgotten memories, the subconscious, and even long-repressed emotions. These, too, are very important to investigate and understand, but they are not the voices of self that speak to you *most* frequently during your *waking* hours, making demands on your time, effort and awareness (sometimes excluding, and sometimes embracing, spirit).

It is not difficult for most of us to understand that our body, emotions and conscience are all parts of ourselves. We can recognise that all of these play an active part in our daily lives. Most of us can also acknowledge that the spirit (or soul) is a part of our nature, but we usually consider it a part of our Sunday lives. We may pray or even meditate daily, but when we finish these activities we go back to our lives as body, emotions and intellect.

The spirit is often experienced as a separate self. It is a self that is confined to times when we are feeling prayerful, contemplative or philosophical. It is a self relegated to occurrences such as Christmas Eves, funerals and weddings. And sometimes it is consigned to global events that tend to lift us out of our individual place in the world and into a communion with humanity – events such as the deaths of John Kennedy and Princess Diana, the Challenger explosion, man's first walk on the moon, and the World Trade Center tragedy.

Still, spirit is what you always have been and who you will always be. Knowing this, you need to help it have a stronger voice in your everyday, moment-to-moment, decision-making life. You do this not by eliminating the other voices in your world but by learning to understand them better so that you can integrate them with the voice of your spirit.

When you keep your intuitive mind involved with all the other parts of yourself and with all aspects of your life, you elevate that life to a level of wisdom, purpose, tolerance and forgiveness that is uncommon in the personal world. On the other hand, if you see your spirit as separate, you will know its peace and its wisdom for only a few fleeting minutes a day.

To create a blending of the intuitive voice with your other internal voices and to experience it more in your everyday life, you must stay conscious of *all* these voices. This may seem challenging at first. Staying conscious is not just noticing what goes on inside your head. Most of us do that pretty well already (sometimes even to the point of obsessing about certain situations or feelings for hours or days at a time). To take consciousness to a level of involvement, you need to speak with these voices, understand what motivates them, and find the hidden messages they wish to bring you.

When Your Body Talks, Don't Ignore It

Often, when we humans first start working with intuition, we have difficulty recognising the experience because we are so greatly in need of 'physical proof'. We want to be hit over the head, tapped on the shoulder, or bear witness to the manna falling from the skies. We seek, indeed crave, physical evidence of an intuitive experience – an experience that by its very nature is spiritual (meaning non-physical). Oddly, though, when we get 'hit over the head' by physical evidence of other types of experiences (emotional, environmental, psychological, etc.), we often carelessly dismiss it with a casual wave.

Isn't it strange that though we are so intent on physical proof, the part of us which is most physical is often the part we most frequently ignore? We often don't rest when we're tired. When we get headaches from stress or eyestrain, we don't necessarily stop what we're doing that's causing the headache but instead pop pills to make it go away. And if we find ourselves with a chronic condition, we simply take stronger pills more often. There is nothing wrong with taking medication to help us feel more comfortable, but often the symptoms we are trying to medicate are the body's attempt to tell us something about our lives, our habits or our feelings.

If we practise listening to those messages and responding to them (giving them the credibility they deserve in much the same way we try to respond to the intuitive voice), then we learn to honour the body rather than dismiss it.

BREAK THROUGH

Ask your body what colour it wants to wear today. Close your eyes and trust the first thing you get. What colour do you perceive? What does that colour mean to you? Now ask your body to 'tell' you one little thing you can do for it today. Will you do it?

If we respond to the little messages of the body when they occur, we can often prevent the body's need to scream at us by creating a chronic or more significant condition. For instance, if your knee begins to hurt when you're jogging, you might put a bandage on for support or stop for a few days to rest your body. If it continues to trouble you when you resume jogging, even with the bandage, do you persist in your jogging programme or do you find another way to exercise? What you do depends on whether or not you are hearing your body say, 'This is not for me', and whether or not you honour your body as much as you honour your belief that jogging is the best way for you to stay fit. Clearly, if your body is hurting, your goal of physical fitness is far from being met. If you persistently ignore such ongoing messages, you may later find that your knee becomes arthritic or you may suffer some other malady that might not have otherwise occurred.

Not all of the underlying reasons for physical ailments are as precise as the connection between hard-impact exercise and a weak knee. Some conditions may be less direct but still result from a physical circumstance or pattern (such as eating or sleeping habits or stress, etc.). Some may indicate a cellular memory of a past trauma, others might reflect repressed emotions or unhappy feelings.

Sigmund Freud had a habit of challenging his family and friends when they bruised themselves, bit their tongues or had other little accidents. Instead of the expected sympathy, he would say, 'I put the question, *Why did you do that?*'⁹

It may be rather annoying if someone else is constantly looking into your emotional and subconscious motives for physical events, but it's probably not a bad habit to develop for yourself. If you think that your body may be holding any repressed or negative feelings, let yourself focus on that part of the body and try to get in touch with the condition. The following is a process that allows you to use your imagery (imagination) to have a dialogue (during a quiet time or in your journal) with a physical condition or with a part of your body.

R E A D Y, S E T, G O !
Discovering the Messages of Your Body

PURPOSE: To establish a rapport with and greater consciousness of the body through imaging and dialogue.

PREPARATION: As always, spontaneity and absolute trust are the keys to a successful experience in this process. And remember to keep your journal at hand.

STEPS:

1. Sit or lie in a comfortable position. Allow yourself to relax as you take a few deep breaths and centre yourself in a space of peace and understanding.
2. If you have a chronic physical condition, or even a mild one such as muscle strain, begin to have a mental dialogue with that part of your body. It may be helpful to imagine that you are writing a script for two characters in a play or a movie. One character, the interviewer, is you; the other is your body.

3. As the interviewer, ask your body (or the specific condition) any question that comes to mind. What is the origin of the condition? What feelings or histories are being held in the cells there? What do you need to learn about yourself? And what action can you take (or what do you need to change) – in your beliefs, your emotions and/or your physical habits – in order to bring healing to the source of the problem and its symptoms?

4. Ask the condition *why* it has come to you. What message is it wishing to share with you? Seek to understand how this message, as uncomfortable as it might be, could actually benefit you by bringing into relief unknown or long-buried issues.

5. For each question, trust the very first spontaneous answer that you perceive. And if you don't get an answer, let yourself imagine one. Remember, you are writing the script between the interviewer and the condition, so make it up.

6. Then ask your body very specifically what you need to do physically, emotionally, and spiritually to relieve and release the condition.

7. Note your responses in your journal, but don't over-analyse. Keep it simple, and keep trying. Pursue any (and every) new physical directive that is indicated and continue seeking an emotional understanding and release.

8. Before completing this process, spend some time visualising a brilliant healing light (of any colour that comes to mind) flooding this area of your body, restoring it to well-being and filling it with peace.

9. Continue these dialogues and visualisations on a regular basis. With practice you will discover your physical-emotional-spiritual connection and the impact that your conscious efforts can make on your health (and your happiness).

OBSERVATION: Sometimes the answers may not be immediately available or easy for you to understand. If this is the case, it is important for you to continue your dialogue with this condition as long as it persists. Unless the condition is structural or genetic, the symptoms will often stop when you 'get the message' that they are trying to convey.

Of course, just knowing the underlying emotional or behavioural connections to the ailment is only the first part of the process. Usually it will require some changes in your physical habits. You will also need a deeper investigation, understanding (and possible release) of past and present feelings and events. Make a commitment to your healing action and to the ongoing investigation of the inner truths that your body holds for you. The next time your body starts to talk to you, even through the most moderate of symptoms, listen to it and take the time to ask it to tell you more.

THE NEXT STEP: Determine to be more attentive to all of your body's needs. Make gradual but permanent inroads into creating a lifestyle that honours your physical experience in every sense. Honouring your physical experience does not mean giving in to your every physical whim and appetite. As a matter of fact, honouring your body requires strong self-discipline. You know what is in your highest good as far as rest, nutrition, exercise and leisure activities are concerned. Make choices not out of duty but out of the joy of giving yourself the best and *becoming the best* in every part of your life.

* * * * *

5

The Ego and Emotion

Recognise the Ego, its Purpose and its Place

When you were an infant, you didn't know the difference between your elbow and your mother's finger. And, frankly, as long as your mother was there to feed you and to keep you warm and safe, you didn't need to know. Alas, there comes a time in every young life when you discover that the warm, fleshy object you keep inserting in your mouth isn't just another toy but your own foot! And thus, the ego is born.

BREAK THROUGH

Quick! In your imaging, your entire body has just turned into one enormous measuring cup. Look inside. How full are you? Close your eyes and look again. Really think about it – *feel* it. How full are you?

(NB: You can do this little exercise frequently. It will always be different and will always help you get in touch with your internal experience.)

The ego is a psychological system within each individual which is governed by what Sigmund Freud called the 'reality principle'.[10] In other words, it is the ego that is responsible for all of the transactions between you and the 'real' world. In this way, the ego is a very good thing – it makes sure you are fed, clothed and warmed (in every way you can imagine). Yet because its singular purpose is to help you get what you need from the physical world, the ego forms all of its definitions in the space and time of that temporary and material world. For this reason, I often refer to the ego as the temporary self or the material self (as opposed to the spiritual self).

BREAK THROUGH

Surprise! You have just won millions in the lottery! Now you can have a collection of houses, the best cars, a personal jet and everything you ever wanted. The winning ticket lies on the table right in front of you. Let go of all other thoughts and worries and again become an enormous measuring cup. Close your eyes to take a look inside. How full are you now?

In its attempt to satisfy your needs, the ego helps you to distinguish yourself from others in order to feed and clothe yourself and keep yourself safe. (It may seem a little silly now, but this was a very important distinction back when they were twenty people in your clan and only one wild boar leg for dinner.) It is a natural, primordial and necessary activity of survival for the ego to divide itself from others. (This part of the ego is also necessary for a healthy sense of self that allows each of us to establish our boundaries.) Yet after centuries of practice in the real-world struggle of humanity, the ego may have taken divisiveness too far. No longer satisfied with something to eat, it has to have the best food. No longer satisfied with a safe, warm place to live, it must have the biggest, most opulent place to live. For many today, the ego measures its success not in the well-being of the individual (as it was meant to do) but in the glamour, fame, money or power it acquires – often through the defeat of others.

This type of divisiveness can be seen not only with individuals, but with countries, cultures, races and even companies and political parties. An example of divisive corporate thinking early in the twentieth century was the White Star Line's slogan to advertise the *Titanic*: 'Not even God can sink this ship'. Not content to advertise the great beauty and wonders of the ship, the *Titanic* had to be better than any other ship – and better than God as well. Yet advertising the *Titanic* as unsinkable was not the largest part of the ego here. Nor were the *Titanic*'s size and opulence. The largest involvement of the ego was the motivation that created the *Titanic* and triggered its sinking – the need to control the North Atlantic shipping lanes and the wealth which that control brought. (For the ego, control equals power.)

BREAK THROUGH

Think about a situation in the last month where somebody hurt you, neglected you or caused you to create an assessment of lack in your life. In the blink of an eye, it is ten years from now, then twenty, then fifty. And, finally, you are one hundred years older. (And in fine shape I might say. The medical advancements have been phenomenal!) What a wonderful life you have had! Think back a hundred years ago. What was that thing that upset you so? How does it look and feel from so very far away? Does it still have the power you gave it so many years ago?

A few other examples in the my-boats-bigger-than-your-boat category are the American Civil War (Southern control of slavery for the perpetuation of the good life) and the tragic Triangle Shirtwaist Factory fire in New York City (management's control of cheap labour for profits).

The pattern in all of these struggles for control is the ego's divisiveness. Somebody's got to lose so someone else can win. The *spirit*, on the other hand, does not divide because it belongs to an eternal collective which embraces all spirit. Spirit *is* indivisible. One part of this collective cannot win if another part is losing.

Since each soul is a member of this unified and ubiquitous mind (Jung called it the collective unconscious), the spirit can never be deserted or abandoned. As an eternal and imperishable being, it cannot be threatened, hurt or wounded. And as a source of divine power and confidence, the soul cannot be victimised, frightened or diminished. Only the ego defines itself in terms of the physical world. Its successes and failures depend entirely upon what it can or cannot accomplish (or acquire) within the limits of time and space.

Since the ego and its world are temporary, loss is assured. Pain, greed, resentment, jealousy, anger and loneliness come – in one way or another – from a perceived loss. (These negative feelings are non-existent to the spirit. The limitless cannot know emptiness. The boundless cannot know lack. In other words, God cannot be diminished, and neither can the divine spark in each of us who is an eternal, loving spirit.) Unfortunately, the difficult emotions which spring from the ego's perception of never having enough are drawn ever larger by its constant need to measure, compete and blame.

It is for this reason that the ego (or the temporary self) may be that part of us which is most obstructive to the experience of the spirit (or the permanent self). Yet, as you work with your intuition, you will become much more familiar with your spirit. You will give your intuitive voice an ever-increasing role in your daily life. And you will happily discover that it is your spirit, not your ego, that tells you what you need from the *real* world.

*In the life of the spirit the importance of
things is measured not by their material
value but by their value to the soul.*

– Leo Tolstoy

The Emotions: How Do You Feel?

Underneath any 'You did me wrong' statement lie the feelings
of sadness and anger. And underneath those feelings lies another
statement: 'I must not be good enough (or valuable enough) for
you to treat me the way I expected.' Ask your inner voice right
now, who really does you the most wrong when you define your
well-being and worth through the capricious actions of others.
Wouldn't you have a greater opportunity for happiness if you
determined your own self-worth? Even when you have difficulty
discovering the grace inside you – which is unalterably valuable
– always know that letting others define you is your choice. If
you don't think for yourself, you will never recognise your ability to act on your own behalf.

When you are overwhelmed by a feeling of anger, hurt or
fear, think first of what possible role the ego (or your temporary
self) is playing in defining this loss. What is the nature of the
measurement of lack? Does that measurement describe your
experience in time or your truth in timelessness?

Embrace the Human Heart

Regardless of which situation triggers negative emotions,
or which perspective adds fuel to the fire of hurt or anger, it
doesn't mean that those feelings are wrong or invalid. The directive here is not to silence, ignore or repress your other voices.
That would be as misguided as ignoring your intuition. After all,
each of our internal voices carries with it an expression of truth
about who we are, where we are going and where we've been
(regarding both our spiritness and our humanness).

BREAK THROUGH

Think about a situation, large or small, in which you were feeling hurt by another. Take a deep breath and go inside for a moment. Look underneath the hurt and anger and find the statement that reflects the lack that this situation makes you feel. Assess the meaning behind each statement. 'He doesn't love me' really means 'I'm not lovable'. 'They don't think I'm smart enough for the job' really means 'I'm not as smart as they are'. Then change the negative 'I' statement into an affirmation – 'I am loving, loved and lovable', or 'I hold myself in high regard in spite of others' responses to me.' Which statement reflects the perspective of your temporary self and which reflects your permanent self? Which perspective will make you the happiest? Can you choose that perspective now?

The intention here is to recognise your feelings, whether or not they are derived from that part of you that lives (and measures) in the temporary world. Whatever your feelings are and wherever they originate, you need to give yourself permission to have them. Denying them or pushing them down because you think they are beneath your experience as a spiritual being will not make them go away. It will only bury them deeper inside you and make them less available to you consciously. These repressed emotions then become yet another message that needs to be brought to your awareness through some other means (such as your body and its health).

In order to embrace the human heart within, you have to

experience and express your emotions fully and seek to understand them. If you're angry or depressed, speak to someone about it or write about it in your journal. Let your words express not just the ideas but the real emotions. Let yourself cry, scream, or punch the couch. If there's another person involved, write a letter and let your pen consume the page with its movement (it's best to wait awhile before deciding whether you want to send it).

Abraham Lincoln believed strongly in the benefits of this therapeutic process. In one instance he advised Secretary of War Stanton to write a scathing letter to a general who had been abusive to him.

'Prick him hard! Score him deeply!' Lincoln prodded.

When Stanton was finished writing, Lincoln told him to put the letter in the stove. 'That's what I do ... It's a good letter, and you've had a good time writing it and feel better. Now burn it, and write another letter.'[11]

Do all your letter writing, pillow punching and journal writing with the intention of letting go, of ventilating your feelings and getting yourself out of the emotional pressure cooker.

Only after you know your feelings,
can you begin to know your spirit better.

All creative and artistic activities – such as painting, sculpting, writing, music and poetry – can be very helpful tools in emotional expression. A newscaster friend of mine has worked with poetry in this way for many years. And when broadcast television becomes too politic and the daily news too toxic, he takes a break through his poetry and makes an 'invisible stop ... where why is never asked.' Of course, for him and many others, poetry not only opens a path to the heart but accesses the soul as well.

Writing poetry may be one of the better methods of emotional catharsis because it is so freeing and so liquid. It provides a great opportunity for spontaneous and moment-to-moment expression. Try it when you feel blocked, off-centre, hurt or angry. Don't concern yourself with form or correctness, just imagine your emotions pouring out of your heart, down your arm and through your hand and your pen onto the page. If you don't want to pursue poetry in a literal sense, simply use your journal for a stream-of-consciousness release. Give yourself over to the process and let yourself truly experience the feelings that come to you.

At first, many difficult, even 'ugly', feelings may come up. Consequently, practising this type of catharsis may seem as if you are allowing (perhaps even supporting) your lower emotions to take over and dominate your experience. But this is only momentary. Purging the emotions in this way gives you the opportunity to *know* your feelings and *release* them (instead of denying and repressing them). If you don't recognise and accept your emotional experience, you are, in fact, rejecting a very real and important part of yourself. You are human, and your feelings matter.

If you make yourself wrong for being human,
you will never be right until you are
no longer human!

So don't push down your feelings because they are difficult, and don't dismiss them because you think they are beneath you or 'bad'. Give yourself permission to be human and to have human feelings. Seek to discover what they tell you about who you are, what you think and how you live. And whenever you make the effort to look at your feelings, take a moment to look at them from your spirit self as well.

Having emotional release is essential to the process of growth and self-understanding. Yet it is by no means the only ingredient. After all, there are legions of criers, letter-writers, punchers and even poets who never progress to the next step of their evolution.

Sylvia Plath, the often introspective and dark American poet, used her poetry as a virtual confessional. It was an outpouring

of her disdain, emptiness and victimisation. Yet, even after years
of poetic emotional venting, she found no other way out of her
pain but suicide. Release is only the start.

It's important to know yourself and your emotional 'make-
up' in a general sense. What are your emotional trends? How
often are you happy, depressed, fearful, etc? These emotional
tendencies can tell you much about whether you are living your
life on purpose and discovering the deeper source of joy within
you.

BREAK THROUGH

Right now, notice a sound in your environment
and really listen to it. Do you find it irritating or
peaceful? Think for a moment about the emotion
of sounds and music. Now, disengage totally
from your surroundings and go inside yourself.
Consider your general emotional make-up. If your
feelings were sounds, what would they be? Would
they tend to be harmonious or cacophonous?
Melodious or strident? Downbeat, upbeat, or all
over the place? Do the sounds of your emotions
wash over you? Or do they spring forth from you?
Take a moment to close your eyes and discover
the melody that is your feeling body.

As you practise to understand your feelings better (and release
those you've been storing up), begin also to engage your intuitive mind. Seek to view your emotions from the perspective of
who you are in eternity. (Looking at your personal life events
from the height of your timeless self is rather like looking back
on the priorities you had in primary school from the perspective
of your adulthood.) What you once thought was mightily

important in the weights and measures of the personal world becomes much more inconsequential to who you are forever.

You have the power to alter your feelings by altering your thoughts and perspective.

If you find yourself brooding about old wounds, mentally reliving a situation that led you to hurt and pain, you are fuelling the negative feelings and will end up keeping the event alive. Instead, stay conscious of your higher mind and live from the heart of your spirit. When an event happens that brings up negative feelings (new or old), respond to the situation not from any lack felt by the ego, but from the overflowing fullness of your spirit. You can do this in the following way: First, *acknowledge and express the emotions* that come up, then see if you can *redefine the situation* that triggered the emotions. *Notice how it reflected the impermanent* aspects of your world. Then *redefine yourself* – in your peace, your permanence and your power. And, just as you allowed yourself to have human feelings, now *ask to know the feelings of your spirit*.

In his book, *Man's Search For Meaning*, Viktor Frankl tells the story of one of his clients, a doctor, whose wife had died. The couple had enjoyed many decades together and the husband was desolate and inconsolable in his loss. After two years of grief Frankl knew that nothing would change unless the old man found some meaning in the event. Then, during one of their counselling sessions, Frankl asked, 'What if you had died first?' The good doctor replied, 'How she would have suffered!' Frankl immediately responded, 'Do you see how you have spared her this suffering?' Suddenly, the doctor's posture changed as he redefined his loss in terms of a higher purpose. He shook Viktor Frankl's hand and left his grief behind him.[12]

Discover Yourself in the Looking Glass of Emotion

Your emotions can provide great insight into your history, your beliefs and your opportunities for growth. Here are three steps to help you see your own life through a deeper understanding of your feelings.

1. Give yourself permission to have your feelings – all your feelings! Don't judge yourself harshly for feeling hurt or angry.

As you build a greater consciousness of your emotions, dismiss nothing that you feel. As a matter of fact, let your awareness sit up and take note of even the little emotions in your experience. First, give yourself an opportunity to express them, and then seek to understand where they come from and what they tell you about yourself and your world. Your emotions are the natural results of your human experience. You have only two options when they come up: you can express them or you can push them down. The second is never more than a temporary response, because if you push your feelings down they will only come up again later. And you will have to make the decision all over again. Feelings that are pushed down over and over will eventually come up in a way which you won't be able to ignore, no matter how much you try.

Don't wait for that to happen. Write about your feelings in your journal. Communicate them to the people involved when you can. Join a box-aerobics class and punch the anger out of your system. After that, try to create a new picture of the situation from the broader perspective of your spirit. See if you can know this situation in a different way.

2. Release your old emotional issues and replace them with a new awareness of the self that realises your future instead of relives your past.
If there is a long-standing pattern of defeating emotions in your life, recognise that a long-term approach of release and restructuring may be necessary to help you discover a new way of feeling. Consider working with a therapist, your pastor, a discussion group or a social worker to help you build this greater awareness.

3. Become more aware that your most joyful moments come from an experience of true inner grace and rarely result from holding up a yardstick to other people's lives.
Unhappy and harmful emotions usually (if not always) arise from a perception of deficiency or lack. Stop comparing yourself to others. Strive to connect with your inner voice (through relaxation, meditation, affirmations, etc.) and practise the feelings of your spirit (tolerance, unconditional love, confidence and forgiveness). These feelings require practice because they are often not the first responses that come to us in the ego's personal world. They are, on the other hand, the responses of the eternal spirit within.

*　　*　　*　　*　　*

6

Reshape
Your Conscience

*The epochs of our life are defined largely ...
by the thoughts that come to us ... that
examine our past and remind us, 'You did
this badly, but you did that and that better.'
And all our future actions serve these former
thoughts and obey their will like slaves.*

— Henry David Thoreau

Freud called the conscience the superego, the voice inside you
that keeps you in line and steadfastly dictates the moral boundaries of your behaviour. Though your conscience can be quite
handy when you find yourself caught in a moral dilemma, it is
actually busiest when it's criticising you! Your conscience notices
everything – your daily activities and thoughts, all the things
you *didn't do* and all the things *you should have said* and *been*. It
chatters perpetually – especially in these modern times – when
self-worth seems to depend on 'making the grade', and achieve-
ment and accumulation seem more important than being.

Our parents were the first to give life to this little voice of
responsibility within us. But most of us have done a wonderful

job as adults – enhancing it, fine-tuning it, shaping it into a world-class athlete who sprints from its perch on our shoulders and leaps into our thoughts the moment we do not meet our own expectations. And, oh, the endurance this little athlete has. It can nag at you all day for the slightest misdemeanour. This is what it's worked for all its life; and like any good personal trainer, it will make you pump the iron of personal guilt until you get in 'superego' shape. And if you resist, it will only add more weight and more repetitions to the programme.

This is the voice of your 'shoulds'. *I should eat better. I should get back to the project that I'm working on. I should pay my bills. I should've spent more time with my son this morning.* And so on and so on. And soooo on! There has often been depicted – in stories, cartoons, and even advertisements – a miniature devil who sits on your shoulder and tempts you to take *wrong* action. If this is true, then the superego (or the conscience) is the spry little *demon of righteousness* who works the second shift.

Your conscience is a demon not because of what it asks you to do, but because of how it makes you feel. Eating right is a good thing. Being organised is a good thing. Spending time with your kids is a good thing. Taking the action to pursue your purpose *is a good thing*! Often, though, something else (like life) gets in the way of completing your list of things to do. Immediately your 'should' voice kicks in, and the first thing you feel is inadequate. Failure and inadequacy are *not* the roads that lead you to take right action or to discover your spirit. But they are a part of the downward emotional spiral that your conscience can create. Here are some steps to help you get out of the negative whirlwind which your 'should voice' propels (and there's not a 'should' among them!).

A List of Things to Do
About Your List of Things to Do!

1. *Change your vocabulary and your predetermined attitude* about the tasks before you.

2. *Alter your experience along with your perceptions* of life – each is the foundation of the other.

3. *Determine the situations you must change* for your own well-being – and change them.

4. Take the time to *open your senses and lift your curiosity* (the way you did when you were a child). In other words, *reassess your priorities* in terms of what's important and not what's urgent.

5. *Find the beauty and value in everything* you do and in the world around you.

Now, this list may seem like hard work, but you will see as we examine each item that it requires only *consistent awareness* and *intention*. With time and practice you will find thoughts of power, joy, opportunity, love and purpose filtering into your daily experience – at first because of your own determination, then out of a growing habit, and finally as a spontaneous response to the new way you've decided to look at your world.

> *Redefine responsibility as possibility and duty as desire. Then you will discover an exciting new day every day of your life!*

This is the way your spirit *wants* you to experience life. It does not want you to wait for your happiness until you've finished your laundry list or until you've worked hard enough for a promotion, or even until the next long weekend. Instead of waiting, you can decide to know real bliss in a quiet (or noisy) moment right now. Open yourself to connect truly with all of the people you meet throughout your day. Feel successful in every step and with every action, whether you're walking on a treadmill, reading a book or even folding a towel. Hold yourself in good esteem, loving who you are even when you get sidetracked. And, most of all, feel alive with enthusiasm for every purpose you hold, from your life's goal to picking up a carton of milk at the supermarket.

Here are all of the items on the list with suggestions about how you can apply them in your life. So, give it a try! You could find that releasing your 'shoulds' just might help you release many self-imposed judgements of inadequacy and feelings of lethargy and defeat. And in the process, you'll discover your list of things to do can become your list of things to love!

1. Change your vocabulary and your predetermined attitude about the tasks before you.

It all starts with the word *should*. Using this word with almost any activity, even beneficial and happy activities, gives you the feeling that you *have* to do it. It becomes an obligation, and obligations always feel more like *work* than fun, even when they are fun. This sets you up for an automatic response of *resistance*, because it is a duty rather than a desire. And resistance means conflict and war, an internal conflict that starts the very first moment you think of the 'should'. Before you know it, you find yourself resisting – and sometimes *resenting* – even the smallest chore on your Should List.

By the way, that the little 'should' devil sits on your shoulder is more than just a metaphor. After all, if you are a good person, you have to 'shoulder your responsibilities' and 'carry your burdens'. As a matter of fact, you'll notice that when your shoulders are aching and your muscles are constricted, your 'shoulds' are talking the loudest and trying to direct your behaviour. This tension often generates through the muscles down your back and up your neck. So if you find yourself experiencing chronic back pain or headaches, your 'shoulds' are probably in the driver's seat. I imagine that it's not a coincidence that the base word for shoulder is should.

Begin by simply changing 'I should'
to 'I want'.

Even this simple change of vocabulary requires consistent awareness and discipline. Sometimes it may feel like a lie to say 'I want'
when you really don't. Yet you can still *employ* concepts of love,
value and happiness in your various activities, even those that
are difficult. Employing these concepts brings you to the next step:
how to *think about* and *carry out* your activities in a new way –
by altering the action not technically, but emotionally.

2. Alter your experience along with your perceptions of
life – each is the foundation of the other.
Please understand that I am *not* suggesting you turn your back
on every personal, social and financial responsibility in your life.
The reshaping of your conscience does not require that you stop
honouring these things, only that you *start redefining your actions
from the perspective of your inner self*. How do you do that?

First, find the joy or happiness or beneficial purpose in all of
the activities on your Should List. Second, start speaking and
thinking about them in those terms. Third, if you can't create
enthusiasm for the task itself, find the joy in its completion.
Fourth, exult in the value that even the smallest activities bring
to your world. Fifth, assign new meaning to *old* experiences. If
you can find the benefit in the present, you can also find it in
the past. This gives you a higher starting point for the future!

Here are some examples. Taking care of Grandma is a great
opportunity for *love*. I *enjoy* how the house looks and feels after
I've cleaned it. I *love* eating healthy food because it gives me
more energy. In spite of the hospital politics, I *want* to be a nurse
because it fills my heart. Even though it's a challenge, I'm taking
classes at the University because I *love* who I am becoming. I am
worth exercising!

In *none* of these statements is there a 'should'. And in none of
these statements is there the perception of obligation. In all of

these statements there is a *gift*, an experience of giving and receiving. So give yourself the gift of recognisisng the benefit in all that you do.

BREAK THROUGH

When you close your eyes, you will see a little 'should' elf sitting on your shoulder. In his hands he holds the hardest task you have to do this week, the one that carries the greatest weight and obligation. After he hands this obligation over to you, you discover the elf is holding something else – a gift wrapped up with ribbon. (Maybe this elf is from the North Pole!) This gift is yours! It comes directly through the first obligation you were given. And this gift – a benefit – is yours only because the first obligation is yours. What is this gift? How does it make you feel? Can you now redefine the initial duty in the light of the subsequent benefit and joy?

You will know far greater happiness in your life if you hold the joy, the value and the benefit of any action more forward in your mind than the time it takes to complete it or the difficulty it imposes.

It takes a lot of conscious attention to stop thinking and speaking about what we must do in terms of heavy obligation. Talking to ourselves with the ever-present 'should' often becomes a long-standing habit that starts in childhood. Yet it doesn't have to be permanent. *If you want to experience more peace than resistance in your life, if you wish to give yourself the chance to bring value and appreciation to even the most mundane of tasks, if you want your spirit to do the dishes, then let the voice of your spirit do the talking. Erase the 'shoulds' from your vocabulary!* Apply the concepts of love, grace, value, enjoyment, purpose, fulfilment and worth to *everything* that you do or even think about doing. Embrace these concepts and use these words, for this is the vocabulary of your inner voice. Again, if there is an ongoing and extremely taxing obligation in your life, you may feel you are lying if you use these words and concepts. But with practice, if you look for joy in even the smallest actions of your day, *you will be successful in finding it.*

There are many demanding, stressful work situations. The business of making a movie, for instance – orchestrating all the details that have to come together – must be considerably distressing. Making the movie *Psycho* must have been (dare I say it?) a nightmare! In a newspaper interview Anthony Perkins once related how Alfred Hitchcock (the director) would stop production on the set for a few minutes whenever things got exceptionally tense. 'Please remember,' he would call out, 'we're supposed to be enjoying ourselves!' (*Los Angeles Times*, 28 April 1985). Hitchcock had a reputation as a stern taskmaster, but clearly there were times when the task was to have fun! The lesson here is not to avoid work, but to learn to enjoy it (or at least redefine it in more enjoyable terms). So, *if your life is mostly about what you can get done, start having it be about loving what you are doing.*

If while you are driving to work, mowing the grass or doing the dishes, you are all the while thinking about the other things you have to do, two results will occur. First, what you are actually doing will become an obstacle to achieving 'the more important stuff', thus creating feelings of resistance and dread. Second, and perhaps more importantly, you will be so preoccupied with what is not yet accomplished (and the tension that brings) that you will not be free to enjoy the task at hand.

3. Determine the situations you must change for your own well-being – and change them.

If there is an activity in which you find absolutely no joy or value, this may be a message that some changes need to be made. Any situation (or relationship) which repeatedly causes you pain or shame is a definite sign that you are not being honoured or respected within that situation.

Be honest with yourself about the relationships and activities that are toxic to your well-being. Determine to change them. Would you buy a house in Chernobyl? Why would you actively choose to invest in your own poisoning?

There can be no room in your life for anyone or anything that makes you feel bad about yourself, belittles you or causes you to feel unworthy, diminished or false to your sense of integrity and grace. And however much you try to justify a 'bad' situation by attaching seemingly important 'shoulds' (for example, 'My husband is emotionally abusive to me, but I should stay for the sake of the children'), you must change it. Any time you choose an activity or relationship which does not honour you, you are teaching people (including your children) that you don't deserve to be honoured. You are sending out a message that it's okay to behave disrespectfully to others, and to allow others to disrespect them.

4. Take the time to open your senses and lift your curiosity (the way you did when you were a child). In other words, reassess your priorities in terms of what's important and not just what's urgent.

The urgent activities that fill our days are *not* usually the important things that fill our hearts. No matter how fast you work or how much you do, there *will always be more to do.*

> *Urgency does not equal importance.*
> *How soon a thing has to be done*
> *is not a measure of its value.*

Try not to fill your life (or your mind) with your urgent Should List – deadlines, projects, meetings, invoice dates and schedules. These will not be the things you fondly remember in your old age. What you will remember are the things that gave your life meaning – the experiences you have valued, the beauty you have known, the individuals whose lives you have touched and those who have touched yours. Creativity, people, music, books and beauty are rarely urgent; so they often come second in our lives. Put them first and recognise their value. Know their importance. *Make* them important – in your life, in your mind, in your heart and, most importantly, in your time.

BREAK THROUGH

Take out your journal or a piece of scrap paper. First, write down the three most important things you must do today. Second, list the three most important people in your life. Third, make a note of the three activities you enjoy most in the world. Study these three lists. Are any items from the second or third list also on the first? If not, why not? Today and every day put at least one item from your favourite people and one from your favourite activities lists at the top of your 'Most Important Things To Do' list. Do this every single day!

5. Find the beauty and value in everything you do and in the world around you.

How do you find the value in everything? After all, it's easy to find the beauty in a sunset and the value in an act of kindness or compassion, but how do you discover beauty and value in the mundane details of life? (Let's face it, 90 per cent of life is spent in the details and not in the sunsets!)

Well, the first thing to do is start noticing the details. Then begin to look for the good in even the tiniest parts of them, and embrace the good that you find there. You will always find good if you look for it! Here is a process to help you find value and beauty in the most mundane parts of your day – your errands.

READY, SET, GO!

Shifting the 'Shoulds' and Finding Value in the Minutiae

PURPOSE: To discover the joy in your life's daily errands (and consequently, in all that you do).

PREPARATION: Determine your willingness to change your mind (and your behaviour) in order to change your life and increase your experience of happiness.

STEPS:

1. *Say* the words. 'I (love, enjoy, look forward to, am happy with, etc.) getting my errands done.' *Decide* to make the words real.

2. Start to enjoy each task using 100 per cent (well, at least 95 per cent) of each of your senses. Notice the *touch* of the leather on the steering wheel during your drive. *Smell* the pies cooling on the rack at the bakery. Acknowledge the muscle tissue you're building while lifting the grocery bags in and out of the car.

3. *Recognise your abundance.* When you're doing routine shopping, buy yourself one little thing that gives you joy. When you go to the bank, instead of impatiently shifting your weight from one foot to the other, take a moment to close your eyes and mentally affirm that all of the money that moves through your hands (and through your account) generates benefit in your life. Consider with gratitude the other riches that are yours, from the people you love to the sunlight that warms your face.

4. *Notice* the wonder of the world around you – the architecture and natural scenes that inspire you, the plants, trees and flowers that enhance your enjoyment of life. Delight in the children, animals and people you meet. How do they share their world with you?

5. *Embark on other journeys* while you're walking or driving from errand to errand. Play music that lifts your spirits or listen to a book on tape. An audio book can give you the world while you're driving to the shops!

OBSERVATION: Observe how you feel when you get home, and *congratulate yourself!* Everything is done, and you enjoyed yourself, too. And now you can drink up the smiles on your kids' faces when they tear into the fresh-baked pastry. And you will hear a meow of 'thank you' when you put down the cat food you bought. This weekend, you can plant the bright yellow mums you bought yourself (and enjoy them for months to come). And tonight you can relax with yourself (or with your sweetie) and let the video you rented conduct you to other lands and other times. But most of all, you can love yourself and your life for all this bountiful joy, and all you had to do were your errands!

THE NEXT STEP: After you've applied this action to your errands, try to embrace your larger obligations in the same way. Start now to catch yourself *every time* you use the word 'should'. Then rephrase your words to reflect your desire (not your duty). If your desire isn't strong, express instead the value that activity brings to your world. Be persistent with this practice. (Agatha Christie always looked forward to doing the dishes because she said it was the 'best time' to write a book. What worlds of mystery can you create while *you're* doing the dishes?)

*   *   *   *   *

7

The Voice of Your Spirit

Give Your Spirit the Title Role

The voice of the spirit is just one of the many disparate aspects of the self that vie for our attention. Listening to it, though, is somewhat more difficult than listening to our other internal voices, because spirit is far more subtle and less familiar to us than the countless clamouring utterances we've been 'hearing' for years. It is the still voice within that comes to the quiet mind, providing a perspective of greater peace than any other voice we have ever known. The voice of spirit directs us to love, usually leads us to understand, frequently asks us to forgive, and always requires us to trust.

Often we hear the intuitive voice, but we let doubt stand in our way. Sometimes we are very clear about what we hear from that voice within, but we may not always like what it tells us, for the spirit is intent upon our growth, even when that growth may be challenging.

The path that the spirit wishes us to follow is the one that leads us to a greater experience of it – to a wider embrace of joy, wisdom, peace and power. These higher emotions – as well as unconditional love, sharing and confidence – all come from the spirit. When you have these feelings, *let yourself really have them!* Dive into them, own them and share them. They are how you feel when you know who you truly are and when your ego doesn't censor your experience of grace. 'The glory of God is man fully alive!' (St Irenaeus).

Your lower emotions, however, come from the temporary self, the only self that can know loss or fear, the lack of love or a lack of respect. On the other hand, self-respect in your thoughts and actions will always lead you to your spirit. And knowing your spirit will always lead you to greater self-respect.

BREAK THROUGH

Quick! Think of the greatest person you admire and respect (living or dead). Close your eyes and really make that personality present with you. Now put that individual in your clothes, in your shoes, in your skin, and even in your head. Completely hold that person in the very space and moment you occupy right now. Ask this person for any advice you need. What one thing would he or she do to make your life better? Will you do it?

Your spirit would never direct you to pain, to fear, to love-lessness or to any activity or relationship which requires you to relinquish your divine and joyous self.

Giving of yourself must never require
giving up yourself.

Your responsibility to others requires a clear and actualised aware-ness of your responsibility to yourself. You cannot know the joy in caring for others if you do not know the joy in caring for yourself. If there is any activity that you do in your life, whether small or large – for yourself or for another – about which you cannot make a statement of love or about which you cannot find some-thing of value, then that activity is probably not directed by your spirit. If there is a relationship in your life that diminishes your worth and extinguishes your joy, then that relationship is prob-ably not directed by your spirit. These situations require you to be awake and to know when you are leading yourself farther away from your truth. These are the instances that call you to act – to make the changes (even when those changes are difficult and emotionally trying) that help you reach that truth and your potential every day.

Creating (and Keeping) an Ongoing Connection With Your Spirit

First, define who you are in the truth of your permanent self and its confidence, love and power.

Second, stop living at the level of *busy. Doing* does not equal being; in fact, it often prevents being. That's why keeping busy is such a good defence mechanism against pain. *Doing* outwardly prevents you from *being* inwardly. *Practise being instead of doing. And even when you're doing, practise being!*

Third, don't take things so personally. Every time you perceive you are being attacked, you define yourself as 'attackable'. This increases your fear and vulnerability and decreases your strength and self-esteem (leaving you even more raw and open to further attack). Set about changing the situations in your life which are truly damaging and practise letting go of the little disappointments that occur only because people are human (just like you!).

Fourth, be sure to meditate or quieten yourself for at least twenty minutes every day. You can't listen to your spirit (or, indeed, to anyone) if you don't shut up first! Make meditation part of your daily hygiene. It will do as much as (and probably a great deal more than) most other routines in keeping you healthy, clear in mind and heart, and stress free.

Fifth, become your own private investigator. Be very aware of all the parts of you which motivate or inhibit you, move you or hold you back. Your fears, your history, your dreams and your beliefs are all compelling forces in your life. To create great change, you must be willing to investigate them and know them intimately. To really know the power of spirit in your life, turn off the automatic pilot and get conscious – of everything you are!

Finally, and perhaps most importantly, *own your responsibility for your own grace, goodness, happiness, purpose, passion and wellbeing*. Own it every minute. Own it every hour. Own it every day!

BREAK THROUGH

The idea of becoming your permanent self may seem a bit too abstract at first. If so, close your eyes and see approaching you the individual whom you perceive as the Divine Being (whoever that may be for you). This Divine personality is here to introduce you to your own eternal self, whom you see approaching now. What do you 'see' when 'look' at your spirit? How do you feel about this self of yours that never dies? Let yourself notice everything (even if it's vague) when you meet your own spirit. What feelings are present?

How Can You Be Sure That It's Your Intuition Talking?

How do you know that your intuitive perceptions are coming from your spirit and not from the ego or your emotional needs? It's really very easy. The nature of spirit is eternal and invulnerable, and the essence of spirit is love. If the guidance you perceive helps to promote confidence, self-understanding and direction in your life, then you can be assured that the source of that information has a link to your divine spirit. If what you perceive brings fear, anger, judgement or blame, then the voice you are hearing is firmly attached to the perishable world and is speaking through a cloud of vulnerability and lack.

The formula for recognising the mind of the spirit is easy: *love* equals *joy* equals *power* equals *spirit*. Evidence of the realm of the temporary is just as clear: *fear* equals *anger* equals *control* equals *ego*. And whether you're working on developing your intuition or making simple decisions in your day-to-day world, it isn't difficult to see which would be the happier directive to hold in your heart and reach for in your life.

So begin now to look for the quality of your spirit's presence through the love and confidence you can feel inside. It is part of the growing relationship that brings you to an easy exchange of ideas between spirit's voice and yours.

Intuition is the voice of the true self. It's what brings you closer to those people, events and life decisions that feed your soul – if you listen to it. Some would say it's the voice of God helping guide you on your own special path that's as unique as your genetic code.

— Allison Abner

Personal Study For Part II

1. Connect more consciously with your body on a daily basis. Make a list in your journal of the choices and new habits that are most supportive of your physical well-being. Refer to this list regularly and take a new step each day to make it real in your life.

2. When you notice any aches and pains, pursue a practice of dialogue with those conditions (as in the exercise on page 53). Be consistent in this. Your body will be with you for as long as you live. Your communication with it needs to be intimate, frequent and enduring. In your journal create three columns, as shown below. In these columns list the physical conditions you experience often (column 1), the emotions which you feel are connected to them (column 2), and the actions you can take to help relieve them (column 3).

———————   ———————   ———————

———————   ———————   ———————

———————   ———————   ———————

———————   ———————   ———————

———————   ———————   ———————

3. Write about your feelings several times a week, especially if you have an experience that triggers hurt or anger. Use some of the writing techniques discussed in Chapter 5 to release the toxic feelings that can poison your life. There are many other emotionally cathartic activities, such as boxing, etc. List some in your journal, and then give those techniques a try. Be sure to write about what happened and how you felt.

4. Stay very aware of every time that you use the word 'should'. Change it immediately. Follow the processes outlined in Chapter 6 in order to experience more joy in all the events that fill your world. Make a list of the 'should' events that you changed today. Write about how differently you felt once you had a new perspective. Also list the 'shoulds' that you could have changed but didn't, so that you can pay closer attention to changing them tomorrow.

5. Keep your spirit mind present in all of life's experiences. Whether a situation triggers your emotions, a physical response, mental analysis or even boredom, ask yourself, How does *my spirit* view this? How does this impact on who I am eternally? What is my response from the whole-of-me, the who-I-am-forever self? In other words, for just a moment pretend you're Charlton Heston in *The Greatest Story Ever Told*. Put on the mental robes of divinity and take a new look at your life. Pick one situation and describe it and your feelings from this new perspective.

*   *   *   *   *

Part III

The A, B, C's
of Applied Intuition:
Ask, Believe, Choose, Detach, Experiment

8

Ask and Answer

Ask, and it shall be given to you;
seek, and you shall find;
knock, and the door shall be opened.

– Matthew 7:7

Inquire Within

You may know a lot of people who talk to themselves. But how many do you know who ask themselves? The distinction between listening and asking marks the first, and perhaps most important, difference between spontaneous intuition and conscious communication with your intuitive self. In both cases, the information is available to you through your inner voice, but in the latter, you are taking the initiative to look for the answers as you need them. (You've always had the answers, you just may not have asked the right questions – or perhaps you didn't even know you could ask!)

This first step opens the door to self-directed communication with your spirit. Asking specific questions allows your intuitive voice to give you answers about specific areas of your life. When you ask your intuition a question, it's important to formulate that question as simply and directly as possible so that there is less chance for confusion when you perceive the answer. After you've asked your question, your intuition can answer you in various ways – with ideas, fleeting images, a gut feeling (as it does during spontaneous intuition), or even by calling your attention to something in the environment around you. Often your intuitive voice will 'speak' to you in visual, verbal or conceptual symbols. What follows is the first and easiest intuition exercise that I teach in my workshops. The symbol is so universal that students from all around the world are able to get it immediately. It's called Red Light/Green Light, and it's just about as easy as the children's game that shares its name.

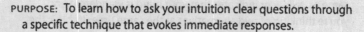

READY, SET, GO!

Red Light/Green Light
The Fastest, Easiest Intuition Lesson Ever

PURPOSE: To learn how to ask your intuition clear questions through a specific technique that evokes immediate responses.

PREPARATION: This process can be done at any time and in any place where you can close your eyes for just a moment or two (obviously not while driving a car!). All you need is your complete commitment to trusting everything that you spontaneously perceive.

STEPS:

1. Think of a situation in your life about which you've been uncertain or ambivalent and then formulate a simple question about it. (Will this relationship bring me joy? Is relocation a beneficial option? Is this new job the best direction for me now?)

2. If you have an 'either/or situation' you need to make two separate questions. For instance, if you want to go back to school and you love both music and writing, ask first about one subject (Would the best course be to take music classes?). Later ask about the other (Would writing classes be beneficial for me?).

3. Hold the question in your mind and imagine a traffic light in front of you. Immediately, as you close your eyes, ask the question and let the traffic signal light up. 'See' whether you get a green, red or yellow light.

4. Trust your first spontaneous perception totally.

5. If you're not a visual person and have difficulty 'picturing' or imagining the traffic light, ask yourself if it's red, green or yellow. One of those words will pop into your mind or stand out for you in some way; so trust exactly what you get.

OBSERVATION: Red obviously means don't cross this threshold, at least not yet. (Even if it's what you want to do, there may be circumstances unknown to you that may not be beneficial. You can ask again at a later date.) Green means go for it. And yellow means wait. (There may be a better option or more preparation may be required.) Red and green alternating either means the same as yellow or indicates that your mind is wandering and you're thinking of two alternatives at the same time. If this is the case, refocus and ask the question again.

You can apply this technique to any situation in your life. Practise it with simple things to become familiar with your own methods of imaging (whether it's words, pictures or feelings).

THE NEXT STEP: Once this exercise becomes easy for you, you will become more comfortable with other symbols as well. The more you do this exercise, the more you will find a variety of symbols popping into your head. This is a sign that your intuition is attempting to provide further information for greater clarity. Keep notes in your journal of these symbols and other symbolic messages you may receive throughout your day (even if you don't fully understand their meanings).

Do not tell yourself 'I'm only making this up' when you perceive the green, red or yellow light. This would be an immediate block to your intuitive success and would not only prevent you from receiving an answer to that specific question, but would also obstruct further work with more detailed intuitive symbols.

BREAK THROUGH

At certain times there may be a situation or a relationship in your life about which you could use some insight. It may be so complex that it sometimes makes your head spin. It seems the more you keep thinking about it, running the same scenes over and over in your mind, the more confused (or perhaps inert) you become. When this happens, for just a moment stop thinking about this entire situation and focus on just one tiny component of it. View one little aspect as if you were looking at a single frame within a movie. Hold the film up to the light to get a better look at the details of that one frame. Although it is two-dimensional and still, much like a photograph, you can see some of the objects or people involved and the positions they hold in the frame. Happily, you have hired a new editor on this film project – your intuition! With a quick splice, your spirit cuts out the next frame and places it in your hand. It is precise and clear. It is almost identical to the previous frame, but one tiny detail is different. What new detail can you add to or take away from this picture that can bring insight? Perhaps someone or something is now out of the picture, or in a different place, or something new has entered the frame. Notice this one little difference between these two frames of your movie. Consider it. It may be a pivotal plot point which takes you in a new direction.

It may take a little practice, but you will find that it is possible to formulate practically anything as a question; and you'll find that you can apply the Red Light/Green Light exercise to many situations in your life. When you have a subject that is too broad to put in a single question, you can compartmentalise it into the components that need clarification. Simply consider all of the factors in a particular situation, and formulate a specific question for each factor. Then weigh the answers, staying ever mindful of how you *feel* with each one.

Sometimes a situation cannot be distilled down to a yes/no (green light/red light), or even to a single concept (as in the movie frame process). A question such as 'What or who is blocking me on this project?' can have many complex and multi-layered answers (my boss, my own fear of failure, a lack of funding, an unconscious desire to pursue other projects, or all of these). It is okay (and ultimately necessary) to ask your intuition these types of questions, but because of the many answers you can perceive, you may find it confusing at first. Let's see what happens.

Think of a question that may have multiple, and perhaps overlapping, answers. Don't try to compartmentalise it or to 'freeze frame' it, just formulate the question in your mind. After taking a deep, relaxing breath, close your eyes and ask your intuition your question about this situation. (Be sure you have your notebook ready.) Open your mind, body and heart to anything and everything you perceive. Many images and ideas may immediately come to mind. Most will be incomplete, and many will not even seem like 'answers'. Your job is to pay attention to everything you notice – every idea, picture, feeling and physical sensation. Notice everything, inside and out, that draws your attention. At first you won't know what to make of these bits and pieces of images or ideas. That's okay; just notice them. And then note them in your journal. After you have collected all of the ingredients for this mixed intuitive salad, take some time to write about the possible meanings of these images and refer to your notes often over the coming weeks.

Don't try to determine a 'bottom line' interpretation for the whole experience. You are simply opening the door.

This is just a sample of the perceptions that can wash over you with complex questions, but over time you will become comfortable with the more elaborate intuitive experience. While you're beginning, though, continue fine-tuning your questions to the basic components for the simplest results.

Questions Not To Ask

1. When starting to work with your intuition, don't ask ambiguous questions that can be answered in conflicting ways (especially 'either/or' inquiries).

2. Try not to ask any 'shoulds'. The question, 'Should I move?' could be influenced by financial restraints or any number of obligations such as those seen in Chapter 6. If you are seeking to remove the 'shoulds' from your vocabulary, don't use them when you're speaking with your intuition!

3. Don't restrict yourself to asking merely about the choices you are *already* considering. There are always more options, and your spirit is capable of knowing a great deal more than you might think. Your expectations may be so hopeful in one direction that you haven't noticed another important alternative. After you have asked about each of your *known* options individually, ask your intuition to show you any choices you may have not yet considered.

4. Stay away from any questions with broad-brush outcomes. For instance, 'Will I be rich?' is entirely dependent upon what that state of being means to you at any given time. Consider all of the different types and qualities of 'richness' that you seek to experience, and formulate a specific question about these.

5. Don't focus *only* on the material outcomes. Your spirit wants to take you to the highest experience of your truth, but it can't take you there if you're only looking for the closest parking space and best retirement package. Ask

your intuition, 'What can I learn from this situation?' or 'How can I make my world better today?' These types of questions will truly make your life richer by helping you discover your power, your purpose and the action you need to take to realise both.

Regardless of the nature of your questions – simple or complex, mundane or profound – the easiest way to open an active communication with your intuitive mind is to ask. *You don't have to be in a state of confusion or have a specific problem in order to ask your spirit to be present.* Indeed, it's imperative that you reach out for an intuitive connection every day *without* having a personal or material agenda. After all, if you're looking to embrace your spirit, then it's up to you to discover *your spirit's* agenda (which in the end is your own higher purpose). Learning to ask without attachment to the outcome helps you look for intuitive direction before your agenda fills the scope of your day. In an odd bit of irony, it is the very act of opening your inner mind during unimportant daily events that can actually lift you out of the personal perspective and into a higher awareness of everything you do. Here is a process that shows you how:

Asking Leads to Opening – All Day!

To create a permanent habit of pursuing your intuitive awareness (in other words, seeking your truth) in all parts of your life, you need to *take that action in ALL parts of your life*. Spend the next two or three days asking your intuition for help with every decision that you make: what shirt to wear, which coffee to buy, which music to play, where to park, which dessert to select, and so on. And when you ask, be sure to take just a moment – a heartbeat – to listen inside. No matter how mundane the question, embrace each answer with a sense of discovery and follow it if it feels right to you. Most of all, appreciate the value of the response and of your deepening relationship with your inner source of guidance!

Obviously, the answers to most of these questions won't be life changing, but the relationship that you build with your spirit through this interaction will most definitely be. Yet in some ways, these little bits of inner consciousness *can* change your life. Though this exercise is meant to encourage more frequent contact with your spirit, it is especially effective if you have fallen into any sabotaging and self-defeating daily habits. Asking your spirit which food to eat if you've been struggling with unhealthy eating habits can be, first, very insightful, and second, strongly effective in terms of changing that behaviour. It teaches you to take time, consider your options, ask what your spirit would do, and then choose the action you wish to take. This practice gives you an opportunity not only to live more consciously, but also to know your eternal perspective – regardless of whether you're eating a potato or calling a friend. *When you choose to know your 'higher' responses, you find that no event is uneventful to your soul!*

You might feel silly asking for intuitive input on such inconsequential matters. But remember, you are not asking these questions because you don't know the answers or can't make decisions. Nor are you seeking information from some externalised source who knows better than you. You are taking the time to connect.

This exercise is for everybody at any stage of intuitive and personal development. For no matter how 'enlightened' we may be, there will always be times when we go through life on automatic pilot. We often become so busy just keeping up, we forget there is a part of ourselves that is greater than the physical and a purpose that is greater than the temporal. With this full-day exercise we can build an ongoing dialogue with our intuition and know its insight more spontaneously throughout our lives.

What a gift just getting a cup of coffee or putting on a pair of socks can be! Our lives are filled with hundreds of these little events every single day. When we invite the inner mind to participate in them, we begin to perceive a weaving together of the outer and inner agenda – as if to say, 'Okay, spirit, what shall we do together today?'

BREAK THROUGH

When people in the physical world want to contact you, they call you and leave a message. You don't have to anticipate their calls or question them in order for them to contribute new information or assistance. All you have to do is check your messages! Take a moment to check in with your intuitive message service now. Close your eyes. There is a desk before you and upon it are a number of messages from your intuition. They don't have to be words on paper. They can be objects, colours, bits of a puzzle, scraps of an idea. They don't have to answer any questions, and you don't even have to know what they mean. All you have to do is look at your desk, 'see' the messages, and notice how you feel with each one. If there is one that seems to confuse you, ask your spirit for clarification – now and throughout your day. (Be sure to stay alert later for any meaningful distractions or spontaneous insights that occur.) Check in for your intuitive messages at least once or twice a day, just as you would for your physical-world messages. They are certainly no less important, and they lend a whole new meaning to the word 'receptionist'!

Now That You've Got the Questions, *How Do You Get the Answers?*

Answers and messages from your inner guidance can appear in many various ways:

1. *Sudden, spontaneous knowing or gut feelings* can grab you right out of the blue. A gut feeling is often experienced as a spontaneous thought accompanied by a sensation of knowing in the pit of your stomach. (This is called 'sentience' or 'clairsentience', which means 'clear knowing'.) Recently, I purchased a home that was unfinished. I wanted to measure the windows for curtains, but I didn't have the key and knew the contractor was working on a different street that day. I decided to go shopping instead. When I got to the corner where I would turn right towards the grocers, I suddenly *knew* I had to turn left to go to the new house. I did so, though I argued with myself the whole way! When I turned onto my new street I saw a truck pulling up to the new house. A carpenter had left his ladder there the day before. I got there at the only moment the house would be open. I took the measurements and was able to order my curtains that day.

2. *Singularly focused, often nagging thoughts* that may stick around for hours, days or even weeks – until you start listening to them!

3. *Physical sensations* can include hairs standing up on the back of your neck, goose bumps, nervousness, butterflies or tightness in the stomach, and dry mouth. My friend Julianne had many of these 'symptoms' one particular day at work. Though work was normal, her hands were shaking, her breath was shallow and she was a nervous wreck. When she got home that evening, she found the front door hanging off its hinges. Her apartment had been robbed that day. (Though these physical sensations are far less common than conceptual, emotional and sentient

experiences, they do occur for some people. It's important to track any physical cues you notice.)

4. *Subtle, undefined feelings of anticipation* can come and go without any necessary stimuli in your environment or in your thoughts, and are difficult to pin down.

5. *Symbols that appear in dreams, meditations and visualisations* that come to your mind spontaneously of their own accord, or *symbols you choose consciously* as focusing tools, just as we have practised in the many Break Throughs and other exercises in this book.

6. *Symbols and objects that you notice around you in the environment* which act as figurative or literal signs, especially when they are repetitive or seem to have a pattern. When my husband was young, he went through a period of several weeks seeing boats all around him. He then decided to build his first boat. After that, the only boat he seemed to notice was the one he was building in his garage! Noticing what's around you and paying attention to what distracts you are important components in experiencing your intuition.

7. *Synchronicity* in meetings, observations, actions and events is a sign that there is no such thing as coincidence!

In almost all of these different ways of perceiving there will be one component that feels the same – a sense of *knowing*. For example, do you remember a relationship in your past that you knew – *knew* – wasn't right for you? No matter how much you made excuses, denied or pretended – the truth, *the knowing of it,* kept buzzing around the back of your mind like a fruit fly around a bowl of bananas. And, in the end, your intuitive voice was right because, of course, it was your truth. Your intuition will always be right because it is that part of you that sees and lives beyond the temporary. (And *everything* in the physical world – from dinosaurs to dental floss, from the Amazon rainforests to amazon.com – is eventually temporary.)

The Difference Between Intuitive Thought and Reasoning

As we have seen, the mind is always active, always set upon one task or another. And even when the mind is focused on intuitive discovery, many other types of thought processes may be happening. For example, you may be *pondering* a symbol and its meanings; you may be *noticing* a sentence, word, person or idea that keeps popping into your head for no apparent reason; or you may be *trying to identify* some vague feeling of expectancy.

All of these activities are 'mental' in some way or another. Indeed, without your powers of *mental observation*, your intuition could no more get a message to you than a radio frequency could get to your house without a receiver. You are the receiver to your intuitive transmitter (your spirit), but how you experience *intuition* is very different from the analysis you use in logic and reasoning.

Since intuition will rarely be about what you think, analysis can actually get in the way of your intuition. Even when intuition comes through a concept or idea, it will be the *feeling* behind it that will indicate the voice of your spirit. For most people it is a feeling that emanates from the heart or solar plexus, regardless of the words or ideas experienced. Your experience of logical reasoning will be very different. Here is an example:

You're going about your day, and then for no reason at all you suddenly think 'I have to call my sister!' You hadn't been thinking about her. You're not worried about her. There are no particular events coming up that you must plan with her. Yet, there it is, a gut feeling to call your sister. You're busy right now, so you put the idea aside. An hour later, it comes to you again, 'I have to call my sister.' This time it seems more compelling – almost as if it were 'louder' inside. The idea has evolved into a nagging thought pattern. And you continue to ignore it. Yet it comes to you all day and even the next (until you do call your sister). And then you discover she needs your input or help in some way. This is the nature of the intuitive voice.

Your logic or reasoning about calling your sister will be decidedly different. Though the thought itself is precisely the same, this time there will be *reasons* for you to speak to her. Perhaps it's your turn to call. Or maybe you had promised her a book which you had forgotten to give her. Or maybe you're just feeling guilty about not reaching out to her for a while. Regardless of the reasons, you will still have the thought many times a day, 'I have to call my sister.' But this time, the repeating thought will feel somewhat tedious or even heavy (regardless of how much you *love* your sister). In this instance, the many reasons to call your sister can pile up like wood by a fireplace or laundry in the hamper. And the feeling is different, too – not in how you feel about your sister, or even *about* the thought. It's different in *how you feel while having the thought.*

Are you compelled emotionally and even physically, almost as if an invisible cord were pulling at your gut or solar plexus? Or are you experiencing this thought in the same way that you experience all the other mundane thoughts that move through your mind in a day? The difference in emotion and energy between these two ways of thinking is significant and distinct. You've had them both, so trust yourself enough to know that you *know* that difference. Make a commitment now to stay more aware of your gut! Notice what *compels* you, and get to know how your own thought processes work. You know which thoughts reflect your truth. Honour them. Your integrity, and consequently your happiness, will depend upon it. (There are other types of repetitive thoughts that can have great emotional content, but they don't compel you to act. They cause you to worry. If you are a worrier and have repetitive thoughts that trouble you, you are wasting energy on a mental exercise that cannot in any way change the outcome of the situation that concerns you. If this is a pattern for you, take a look at Chapter 14 to find some ways to release your worries.)

Symbols and Signs

In 'How Do You Get The Answers' we took a look at spontaneous knowing, thought patterns, and even some of the physical responses that can accompany gut feelings. *If a sense of knowing reflects the Presence of your spirit, then symbols and signs reflect its Language.* Symbols can be experienced in your waking consciousness, daydreams, subconscious, meditations, dreams, drawings, doodlings, environment, and even in a song connected to a special memory. Symbols can come to you as concepts, images, words, ideas or pictures. You can 'see' them in your mind's eye; you can image them in your imagination; you can hold them in your mind as a thought or a concept. The perception of symbols can vary from person to person, and from time to time for each person.

Usually, the intuitive experience of symbolic messages can be very fleeting and incomplete, as if someone has thrown you a few pieces of a puzzle without giving you the box with the picture on it. Yet the process is not as enigmatic as it may seem. You don't need a Rosetta Stone to decode the symbols from your spirit. *Since your spirit knows you, it will speak to you in a language you know, in ideas and images that are already a part of your consciousness.* Your intuitive symbols will not be in the form of ancient hieroglyphic texts, obscure constellations or undecipherable code (that is, unless you are an archaeologist, astronomer or cryptographer).

There are three primary types of symbols:

- personal symbols
- universal symbols
- symbols in the environment

Personal Symbols

As you have seen through the processes in this book, symbols can provide much intuitive insight. Many of the symbols you perceive through intuition will be personal to you. If, for instance, you perceive a symbol of a rose during an intuitive experience, it could signify romance. On the other hand, if you are a student of (or have a curiosity about) the War of the Roses, this symbol may indicate a confrontation or inner battle that needs your attention. As you learn what your own symbols mean to you, note them in your journal. Just remember also to note the *feelings* you had when you perceived the intuitive symbol – not just an analytical interpretation.

Sometimes it's difficult to believe that a recollection of a book you just read or a scene from a movie you recently saw could act as intuitive information. Since it is something in your immediate experience, there is a tendency to think that the symbolic message comes not from your inner guidance but from your imagination or simply your recall. Remember, though, that your conscious mind – including your memories, interests and areas of study – provides the best language though which your spirit speaks to you. Absolutely everything that you experience, learn, read or study –a painting you've seen, cookery classes, ideas for a project – is a potential personal symbol. So the more you learn, the more your spirit has to draw upon. You can tell that a symbol comes as a message and not a memory by the *feeling* that you have when it comes to mind. Do you feel it has a deeper meaning? Does it feel compelling in some way, even if you don't understand quite how? When you notice such feelings, be sure to notice the symbol – and everything about it.

Universal Symbols

Many symbols are more universal than personal in meaning. Some are social, cultural, generational or even religious in nature. (See Appendix B for some universal symbols.) An image of a coin will usually mean money, finance or investments for most people. A bird in flight often indicates freedom. White means purity. Red roses mean love, and so on and so on. Sometimes a universal symbol can become a personal symbol through personal experience with that image. (For instance, birds in flight were an obsession for Leonardo da Vinci, who designed many instruments of flight.) For this reason, it is important to become aware of your own unique, personal interpretations of symbols. This is one reason an intuition journal is so valuable; it gives you a chance to note the symbols you experience and all the possible interpretations that come to mind now and over time.

Symbols can also be literal or figurative. I once had a client who began to 'see' For Sale signs every time he fell asleep and frequently when he meditated. Though he hadn't been thinking about moving, this repetitive message caused him to start considering it. He sold his house and moved to a new neighbourhood which he liked very much. The following year there were heavy rains and the Mississippi River overflowed its banks, flooding vast areas in many states, including his old street.

The For Sale sign is an example of both a universal symbol (meaning a potential move for most people) and a literal symbol ('Sell your house now').

Symbols in the Environment

Symbols in the environment occur when something you see around you catches your attention and you *feel* that it carries a message from your spirit to you. Even a distraction can lead you to more information. If, for instance, you open your eyes during an intuitive process and are strongly distracted by an object in the room, that object could actually be part of the message. Whatever draws your attention in your work-a-day life (and in your meditations and intuitive exercises) does so for a reason. Anything that may seem like a distraction should be noted and considered within the context of your life's challenges and opportunities. If you have difficulty applying an interpretation to any environmental symbol, at least note it in your journal for future reference.

I am reminded of a story about an acquaintance who had been deliberating about going to a college where most of the faculty were nuns. The entire time that this was on her mind, she kept seeing nuns everywhere, in restaurants, at the bank, in the shops. Even a licence plate on a car in front of her at a stop sign contained three numbers and the letters NUN. When she finally did enroll (after many repetitions of this message), the plethora of nuns seemed to vanish from her environment!

Of course, many women know that when they start thinking about having babies, they start seeing babies everywhere. Other people might say that there are always babies out there, and that these women are only seeing them now because pregnancy is on their minds. That may be true, but perhaps pregnancy is on their minds because that is the direction their spirit wants them to take. And they are noticing the babies now because their spirit is pointing them out.

It is the intention of the intuitive mind to use your environment to give you messages. Obviously, the objects that it shows you are already in your environment. Your spirit doesn't create physical objects and put them in your path so that you can trip over your message. It calls your attention to them by distracting you with a sense of their significance or the frequency of their appearance. You will know when something around you acts as a symbolic message by the way you feel about seeing it, the way you feel when noticing it.

You can even *ask* your intuition for a sign in your environment. Just hold a specific question or situation in your mind and simply ask to be shown through the day those symbols that will help you with this problem. All you have to do then is be aware of what you notice.

Or you may want to take an even more direct approach. A friend of mine had been labouring over a difficult situation in her life. She had been loaning money to a relative whom she thought truly needed her help. But after some considerable time, it didn't seem that her relative was making any attempt to become more self-reliant. She felt really painted into a corner. Finally, she threw up her hands in frustration and said, 'Should I keep loaning him money? I want a sign now!' She spun on her heels and looked out the window immediately in front of her.

Her eyes fell instantly upon a stop sign at the corner! There were dozens and dozens of other objects, both in the room and outside, at which she could have looked, but she didn't. She quite literally got her sign – her STOP sign!

BREAK THROUGH

Think about a situation or problem and hold it in your mind. Close your eyes for a moment and ask for insight. When you open your eyes again, let your gaze fall on one simple object. This will tell you something about the situation. See what insight you can discover in your environment when you open your eyes. (You can also practise this throughout your day. Just notice the first thing you see when this situation pops into your mind. What does it tell you?)

You Know More About Symbols Than You Think!

Symbols are far less enigmatic than many people realise. There are dozens of books about the meanings and origins of all kinds of symbols – dream symbols, religious symbols, historical symbols, all types of symbols. Fortunately, though, you probably already understand the images your intuition uses because it is *yours*. You can study these different types of symbols if you want to widen your understanding of the many interpretations they carry, but when you're working with your intuition you must always ask yourself first, 'What does this symbol mean *to me*?'

Usually, the answer you get will be obvious. Symbolic images are often quite literal. Stop signs mean stop. Babies mean babies. Coins mean money. And even nuns mean nuns! Yet symbols can be figurative, too. Babies can mean new life and rebirth. And coins can reflect investments, income and jobs as well (sources of income).

Even when images are metaphorical, you know more about them than you think. If you hear about a person who 'sees the glass half-empty' you know immediately that person has a pessimistic attitude. Symbols as metaphors are everywhere. They are used by everyone to communicate the many conditions of work, love and life that we all meet every single day.

She's over the moon. Don't rock the boat. Go for the gold! We'll cross that bridge when we come to it. He's under the weather... over the hill ... in hot water. You hear these statements (and dozens like them) many times over, and never once have you thought that boats, bridges, hills or water were actually involved. Nor did you think, 'I don't know what that means.'

Yet when we are first learning to work with our intuition, we are often very hesitant to trust what we already know about symbols. Because intuition is new to us, we might think the symbols will also be new (and some certainly may be). Or since we are moving into a deeper understanding of ourselves, we wonder if the symbols will carry deeper and more abstruse meanings (and, again, some of them probably will). But I think the main reason we are so tentative about the symbolic messages from the spirit is that intuition itself is such a subtle and tentative experience. Still, just because the actual 'sensing' of intuitive perceptions can feel very ambiguous at times, it doesn't mean we have to fill the message with ambiguity. Whatever you live, learn, think and enjoy will bring you symbols. For instance, if you love music your spirit will speak to you through music. The bottom line about symbols is this: Whatever any symbol means to you in your normal, everyday world will probably mean the same in your intuitive world. So trust what you already know. Write about your symbols in your journal, and notice how their interpretations grow and change over time.

Dream a Little Dream!

One area where you are probably quite familiar with symbols is your dream life. You can practise working with symbols more consciously by 'redreaming'. Choose a dream which is very familiar, comfortable and strong for you. Recall it as completely as you can. Then close your eyes and recreate it in your imagination from beginning to end. See it, feel it, taste it, smell it. Be *in* it as fully and completely as possible. And simply notice all of its symbols.

Since this is a dream, you don't have to wonder if it makes sense. It can go in any strange direction it wants, and it doesn't have to mean anything in particular. It is a reflection of your own mind, and as such is valid. Seek to experience the dream fully and richly; and if you can't recall it in its entirety (or if you can hold only a part of it in your mind), then pour yourself into that part. Notice every detail and feel every emotion.

Once you've practised this with a dream you've had, ask your intuition for a waking dream that can give you information to help you now. Close your eyes, look for a symbol and pretend you are dreaming about it. Allow it to expand, change, grow and take you through an evolving story. It doesn't have to make sense. You don't have to second-guess your impressions. You don't have to question the mini-dream's validity. There is no right or wrong. All of the images in your dreams and intuition – though subtle and sometimes surrealistic – are valid because they seek to inform. Notice what they tell you and how you feel. Take a few notes about your experience in your journal.

READY, SET, GO!

Reading the Signs and Symbols

PURPOSE: To practise the inner experience of symbolic messages
and become more familiar with the language of symbols.

PREPARATION: A few deep breaths to prepare for a deep relaxation
process.

STEPS:

1. Close your eyes and relax your body, muscle by muscle, as you
   continue to take easy breaths. Feel the presence, peace and
   confidence of your spirit. Open yourself to 'see' or sense an image.
   Ask your inner guidance for just one symbol that can bring you
   insight. (If you wish to focus on a particular question, you may.)
   Don't create blockages by thinking *I don't know how to do this* or
   I'm not seeing anything. Use your imaging to 'see' or know
   whatever symbol pops into your mind. (See your symbol just as
   you would if I were to tell you to imagine a green apple.) Trust
   what comes to you, and if nothing comes to you, create
   something!

2. Keep the experience simple. Stay focused on that one symbol;
   and if your attention wanders, simply bring it back. Watch that
   symbol and get all the information you can about it. Where is the
   symbol located in your perspective? What is its colour and size?
   Place yourself *inside* the experience of the symbol and *notice how
   you feel*. Imagine you *are* the symbol (in other words, how do you
   feel as the green apple?). What are your emotions?

3. After your initial observation, ask your intuition to animate the
   symbol and *watch the symbol take action* (for example, watch the
   green apple drop, fly, shrink or grow). Notice how your symbol
   moves or changes in any way. Later write about these changes
   and what they might mean to you in your journal.

4. As you watch the action of your symbol, let yourself experience
   the feelings of the action. This may seem silly at first, but
   remember, feelings speak volumes in intuitive work. Here's an

example: If your symbol is moving upwards in your 'vision', note whether the movement is quick and exultant, slow and difficult, or perhaps slow but purposeful. Note how the action itself *feels*.

5. Sometimes the image changes into an entirely new symbol, or other images begin to come into the picture. Let whatever happens happen, and consider each aspect of each image by placing yourself inside the symbol and in the action.

OBSERVATION: This exercise is somewhat like the process of focusing on a movie frame by frame to discover the course of action to be taken. In this case, though, you are narrowing the focus even further to just one object within the frame. And you are paying more attention to the feelings. (Even when you're considering action, your focus is the feeling.) The importance of the emotional content here is twofold. It teaches you to pay better attention to your *gut* feelings when you see or perceive a symbol (in your inner work *or* in the environment). And it teaches you to look at symbols from all angles, especially from the inside, with a first-person perspective of how it feels.

THE NEXT STEP: Continue to notice all of the symbols in your world. And be sure to write about them (and about this exercise) in your journal. Your work with these signposts now will help you take advantage of the symbols in and about your future.

*   *   *   *   *

Tips for Asking and Answering

1. *Release doubt. Always trust everything you get, and always trust the way that you get it.* Your mind, imagination, body, memory and even the physical world around you are all available to your intuition so that it can bring you insight. Don't despair that you're just imagining things or making them more important than they seem. *Imagining*

*is your source of imaging. It's how you see inside, or how
you get your insight.* So be confident with your symbols,
words and images. And don't minimise the opportunity to
discover a depth of meaning in everything in your life.

2. *GO DEEP!* Listen deep, see deep, feel deep and go deeper.
Your truth lies deep inside you. For many, it is buried so
deep they don't recognise the falsehoods in their lives. *Go
to your truth!*

3. *Embrace your intuitive experience even if you don't
comprehend it.* An idea can drop into your mind as gently
as a butterfly lights upon a flower. It could be in the
flicker of a moment or in a recurring thought. It could be
a feeling that comes with an indistinct symbol.
Remember, perceiving intuitive symbols is often like being
sent a puzzle one piece at a time. Little may make sense
at first, but to get the whole picture you must embrace
every piece as it comes, as soon as it comes.

4. *You can get the answers without knowing the answers!*
Everything doesn't have to make sense all the time. In
fact, it won't! No matter how much you use your
intuition, there are going to be times when you're not
sure what the images, feelings or perceptions mean.
Sometimes we need to wait for events to unfold to find
their meaning. And sometimes it's a question of building
trust, continued self-discovery, and letting go of the
results (which we will look at a little later).

5. *Get to know your own style of seeing inside.* There are
many exercises in this book and many that you will create
over time. Each individual will experience each process
differently. Experiment with your own techniques and
become comfortable with them. And remember, even
your own methods of perception may change and grow
and evolve. Stay flexible. Invite new ways of seeing.

6. *Keep practising.* Learning the language of your spirit is
like learning any new language. If you don't think it feels

successful at first, remember that practice takes time and repetition. Any pursuit of value is worth your long-term commitment and your effort.

7. *Diversify your practice. Play with the possibilities.* Even though you wish to know your own intuitive methods, play with different techniques, too. You may be a very visual person and perceive symbols through mental pictures, like I do. Yet there are many other ways to perceive – through gut feelings; 'hearing' or thinking words and ideas; sensing images visually or conceptually; physical sensations; sudden insights; feelings and emotions; spontaneous memories from your history; symbols in your environment. You don't have to develop a repertoire. Just open yourself to the possibility of new ways of 'seeing'.

8. *Wake up to the details.* Notice every little thing! If there are no details in the image or symbol that you're experiencing, create them. Don't analyse details, become them! Know the details completely!

9. *Notice what is calling your attention inside and out.* Your intuition will call to you, so notice what feels *significant*. Stay alert for what grabs your attention, and then give it *more* attention! Let the idea grow.

10. *Live in a state of curiosity!* Wonderment and discovery encourage the pursuit of the soul.

11. *Ask and Answer!* Create questions about everything, either for your intuition or just to satisfy your curiosity! Write your questions in your journal. If you don't get an answer, create one. Imagine it. Image it. Whenever you ask a question, get in the habit of answering it immediately (both in your intuitive work and in your life). This builds the habit of trusting your very first spontaneous response. And it helps you remember that *all the answers are already inside you!*

12. *Be willing to release your agenda and go where it may be difficult to go.* Often, answers can tell you more than you ask or tell you something you don't want to 'hear'. Don't reject the information you receive because it challenges existing conditions in your life. Remember, being ignorant does *not* equal being safe.

Knowledge is the accumulation of facts and information. It is the storehouse of data you have already learned. *Knowing* is the action of comprehending – comprehending what's in your head, in your heart and in your soul. Because of your intuition, your *knowing* can be about anything, regardless of data learned. If you are ever in a position where you must decide between your knowledge and your knowing, choose your knowing! Trust your knowing. Seek your knowing!

Always Seek Knowing.

Always Seek Knowing.

Always Seek Knowing!

9

Believe

People only see what they are
prepared to see.

— Ralph Waldo Emerson

Believing is the second important component in applied intuition. Nothing happens in your intuitive experience (or even in your life) without your belief that it can happen – more appropriately, your belief that *you* can make it happen. There are two things you must do uncompromisingly if you want to work well with your intuition:

- Believe in yourself.
- Believe in your intuitive perceptions.

Of course, believing in your intuition is rather like believing in yourself because your intuition is the voice of your true self, your spirit. Though these two actions of belief obviously overlap, let's take a look at both to see how they build the highest experience of your inner awareness and your absolute potential.

Believe In Yourself!

It seems that self-esteem issues trouble almost everyone to some degree these days. A life of confidence, power and grace can only be built upon your belief in that power and grace. Yet that can be a challenge for us humans in this world of competition and criticism. The highest belief in the self requires belief in the eternal self. We'll take a greater look at this in Part IV. For now, let's just take a brief look at the impact of belief.

BREAK THROUGH

There is a treasure chest in front of you. Inside it you see all the parts of you that you treasure – your traits, habits, qualities, gifts, talents, everything. Take a moment to close your eyes, lift the lid and look inside. Recognise everything about you that you treasure. Say 'thank you' for these valuable parts of yourself. Now notice what is *not* in the treasure chest. Can you change your mind and embrace some of the things you previously didn't value? What do you need to do in your beliefs, your actions, your life, to be able to place *every* part of yourself in your treasure chest? Can you simply choose to do so?

Your first and most important job in life is to know yourself: what you want to do, what you have to heal from your past, who you want to become now, and how you can best honour yourself and your world. Your spirit can help you discover these answers, but *you* must do the work. First, define yourself as spirit. Second, believe in yourself as spirit. Third, act with the determination and will of your spirit. Here is a process to help you capture that feeling, even if just for a few minutes. (That's how we open the door to the experience of this true self, just a few minutes at a time.)

Take a moment to think back to the most sacred experience in your life. Where were you and how did it come about?

Perhaps you were inspired by a piece of music, or lost in a moving poem or a prayer, or struck by the majesty of a mountain peak.

As you recall this moment go inward and recreate the sanctity and grace you felt at that time. It may be difficult at first to have the feeling of beauty without the external stimulus, but keep trying. Take a few very deep breaths, and with each inhalation breathe in the absolute serenity, peace and calm you remember from that event. Keep going deeper. With each breath, go deep within that grace and calm – so deep within it that the external stimulus is no longer relevant. As you breathe in that beautiful, glowing peace, feel it fill you and move through you. Allow that absolute peace to penetrate every level of your consciousness and being. Believe in it; this is the nature of your true self! (Practise this exercise often. It's much easier to believe in your potential when you recognise your power.)

Believe or Make-Believe

One of the biggest problems we have in believing our intuitive perceptions is that we feel we're 'only imagining them'. This is valid to a degree. It comes from a lifetime of using the imagination to go to places that aren't 'real', through daydreams, fantasies, pretending and wishing. But your imagination is not some invalid part of your mind that serves up only falsehoods and flights of fancy. It is the part of your brain (the right brain) where you 'see' things, where you experience pictures (as opposed to your left brain, where you process words, data and analysis). Remember, *the imagination is quite literally where you image.* It's where you process visuals, whether from an advertisement in a magazine or from your intuition. What a shame it would be to disregard all intuitive images just because they are images (and therefore move through the imaging part of the brain). Your imagination is a tool of communication derived from many parts of yourself, including your intuition and your unconscious. Take advantage of this great tool. Don't diminish its value;

utilise it. When you get a message from your intuition, don't think you're 'only' imagining it. Instead, *image it!* See it in your mind's eye and hold the concept in your thoughts. Let yourself see, then trust what you see!

Another diminishing sentiment that undermines belief in intuition is, 'It's only make-believe'. For many people that sentence usually means, 'It's only pretend.' Yet perception of your intuition absolutely requires you to 'make believe'. Because, in its truest sense, using your intuition is *making yourself believe* – in yourself, in your 'extra' senses and in the validity of your intuitive experiences. So whenever you have a doubt, *make yourself believe!*

To Believe in Your Intuition, USE IT

Intuitive perceptions are indistinct by their very nature. They don't belong to the physical world. And, since we are physical, we tend to disregard experiences that aren't measurable in those terms. We often doubt and second-guess the subtle messages we get from the intuitive mind, especially when we're first starting out.

When you begin to communicate consciously with your intuitive mind, it is helpful to have hands-on experience of observing the symbols you perceive. This helps to make the experience more concrete for you. This next exercise helps you build your powers of observation by giving you a physical cue that you can carry throughout your day.

Card-Carrying Observer

Choose a word or phrase that represents a challenging, curious or confusing situation in your life, and write it at the top of a blank index card. It could read: My *relationship with ....;* *my job change; my career purpose;* and so on. Take a moment to look at the card and give yourself the suggestion that every time you touch the card today, your intuition will share some insight about that situation with you. Make a mental commitment that this card will trigger an intuitive response *every* time.

Then put the card in the top of your purse, a pocket, your briefcase, or a desk drawer that you open frequently. Every single time you touch the card, write the very first word, idea or feeling that comes to mind. Don't write paragraphs, just a single word or two that encapsulates the feeling or idea you perceive in that moment. If you don't automatically get an insight when you touch the card, create one. It could be anything that grabs your attention mentally or in your environment. By the end of the day, your intuition card will be filled with unrelated words and phrases, some of which may not seem to have any connection to the 'title' at the top. (Your card might read: blue, car, stop, love, spring flowers, happy, desk, exit, up, etc.)

Before you go to bed, take a look at all the words you have written on the card and apply each one in turn to the situation. Add each word to the 'title' and see how it changes the concept. Consider how each word might apply to the situation both literally and figuratively. Most importantly, see how you *feel* in each case. Write in your journal about what you discovered during this process, and don't worry if each and every word on the card doesn't fit with the situation. Some will definitely be revealing – clarifying your course of action and allowing you a deeper understanding of your feelings about the situation.

Keep the card in your journal and look at it again in a week. You may want to do the 'observation card' process with this same situation after some time has gone by. You can also do it with other issues. Just be sure to take some days off so that you don't desensitise to the trigger (the card). And be sure to do only one card per day to avoid confusion. You may even want to try a card with the title 'my intuitive awareness' and see what you get!

Do this process every now and again to hone your skills of spontaneous observation. The steps are simple: always anchor in your mind the suggestion that you will have an intuitive perception *every* time you touch the card. Keep the card in a 'hot spot' where you will come across it frequently. Write an immediate perception when you do come across it. At the end of the day, take a look and consider your perceptions. Return to your observations intermittently over time to discover any new feelings and insights. Keep this simple! If you make this process a big deal, you won't do it. It will only take a few moments, but it can have a big pay-off in your practice of observing and believing!

Now, here is another exercise that helps make symbols more real for you.

READY, SET, GO!

Show me a Sign!

PURPOSE: To designate a symbol which can represent a particular situation and bring you messages from your intuition.

PREPARATION: Think about symbols. Just as you would turn to the 'R' index tab in the dictionary to find the words beginning with that letter, you can designate a symbol to represent any situation, condition, or even an interest, in your life. To prepare, all you have to do is consider the matter about which you would like guidance from your inner voice.

STEPS:

1. Identify the situation in question, such as a relationship issue, your studies, a challenge at work, a needed change at home or in your career (even if you're not precisely sure what steps that change entails), or anything that's important to you. Think of the words that would best and most precisely identify the situation in your mind.

2. Once you have identified the situation, create a symbol that can represent this situation for you. The symbol does not have to describe the situation, but should just be something you decide will be your sign from the 'universe'. It should be singular enough to stand out for you, yet not so common that you would see it hundreds of times a day (such as a tree). Choosing a common image in a unique colour is one way to make it your own (such as a green heart, a red feather, a pink letter, a purple door, a blue

shoe, etc.). Names, words, or less common objects would also work.

3. After you have chosen your symbol, make a note (or even a drawing) of it in your journal, along with the words that best identify the situation (as you had determined in step 1).

4. Take a few minutes during your meditation to focus on your specific symbol and open yourself to perceiving anything that comes to mind, remaining constantly aware of your feelings as you do so. Note the experience later in your journal.

5. Every morning when you awake, remind yourself of the situation and its corresponding symbol. Close your eyes for just a moment and anchor that image in your consciousness. Affirm that you will stay alert for *every* occurrence of that specific symbol in your environment.

6. When you do see your designated symbol, notice *everything* about it – where you see it, *what you were thinking or feeling when you did*, and what things or people stand out around you. Either write about these experiences in a notebook as you make these observations or note them in your journal later.

7. Every time you make an observation in your journal about your experience of that symbol, make a drawing of it in the margin so that you can locate that notation easily. After a few weeks, look back over all your notations and consider the overall message your symbol has been providing. (Don't be surprised if, during this time, you experience the symbol in a way that provides an immediate revelation.)

OBSERVATION: Sometimes you may already have a feeling about the action you need to pursue in a particular situation, but you just want a 'sign' that it is the right time for that action. Just decide what that sign is and ask to see it around you. (You may be surprised at how often or how significantly your chosen symbol begins to show up in your life, even if it's in an uncommon colour.) If there is an absence of that symbol, that is a message too.

THE NEXT STEP: With practice in staying conscious, you will become more comfortable with noticing symbols in your environment. You can then start to play with it a little more. You can even designate a symbol that represents your own spirit. Then every time you see it, pause for a moment and notice that your intuition is calling. After you've taken in all that's around you, close your eyes and go inwards. Take the call from your intuition! Just ask, 'What do you want to tell me?' And then 'listen' for the first thing that comes to mind. This helps to open a direct line of consciousness to your intuition.

* * * * *

Steps in Building Belief in Yourself and in Your Intuitive Experience

1. *Recognise the part of yourself that is larger than who you are merely in time and space.* (We'll take a look at the techniques to do this in Part IV.)

2. *Don't criticise yourself.* Appreciate who you are and what you have. When you know that all you need is inside you, you become free to meet your destiny.

3. *Hold yourself in high enough esteem to value your experiences and observations.* If you validate what you notice, you will be open to notice more.

4. *Build your skills of observation and notice everything –* even what you say by accident. You'd be surprised at how often your intuition 'puts words in your mouth'.

5. *Trust yourself.* Trust your gut instincts. Trust what you know. *Know what compels you.*

6. *Stay mentally relaxed.* You can't be receptive to the guidance and peace of your spirit if you spend your life only in reaction mode.

7. *Practise seeing and thinking in symbols and concepts.* When you experience your world (even the smallest things), be as synaesthetic as possible. (For example, visualise the colour of jazz.)

8. *Pay attention to repeating symbols and themes* in your dreams, in your intuitive imaging processes and in your environment.

9. *After receiving a message, translate it but don't analyse.* Remember, there's never a wrong image – only a mistaken interpretation. Consider *all* possible interpretations, and stay open to new meanings that may evolve over time. Regardless of how you interpret the possibilities, the answers you seek *must ring true*. They must feel true in your heart and in your knowing. If they don't, keep looking.

A River Runs to It

Here is a process for tapping into the flow of energy and information between your intuition and you. There are no questions to ask, no answers to get. Breathing, relaxing, imaging and experiencing are all that's involved here.

Close your eyes and take a deep, relaxing breath. As you invite the presence of your spirit, begin to notice a small, peaceful, gently flowing river of light in front of you. Let yourself *image* it exactly as it comes to you. With the next deep inhalation, and with every inhalation thereafter, the river of peace flows directly into you. And with every exhalation the river flows out, like a tide of light ebbing and flowing, coming and going, in and out. Take a moment to simply let this river of light, energy and imagination flow back and forth, back and forth, with perfect ease and comfort. After a few moments of this gentle exchange, you begin to notice that floating in this river are many, many small symbols. There are shapes (from triangles to circles); forms (from stars to hearts); objects (from books to toys); and even numbers, feelings, and letters of the alphabet. Notice these little symbols bobbing gently up and down, just peeping up out of the water as it comes and goes with every gentle breath. Allow anything and everything to come to you, but don't ask any questions or look for any answers. Just be in the flow.

Let the symbols, the comforting energy, the beautiful light flow in and out, back and forth. Easy, so easy; the guidance and peaceful strength flow with every breath from your intuitive self to you and back again. Enjoy it. Employ it. And *believe* that your ability to know the mind and the heart of your spirit is as easy and as natural as breathing.

Don't Block Your Believing

One of the best ways to increase your belief in signs and images is to become a seer! Even if you're not a predominantly visual person, begin to practise seeing things with the mind's eye. Read authors who tend to be visual and highly descriptive. Notice details everywhere, and look for the deeper value in even the little things in your life. Keep a dream journal to discover the images that come to you in dreams, and practise imagery in your meditations. Study and investigate anything and everything. New learning broadens your vocabulary of symbols. Remember, though, the perception and interpretation of symbols are not the ends but the means. They challenge you to find the deeper meanings of life and the deeper value within you.

Even though opening to new areas of interests helps to broaden your vocabulary of symbols, don't fall into the trap of over-reliance on getting informed instead of trusting your knowing. Regardless of what the technological world might say, science and reasoning can take you only so far. Computers and robotics already surpass man in many activities and calculations. They play better chess, they encrypt codes more easily, and scientists are now even programming computers to make interactive decisions. Yet machines will never be able to intuit. They are not self aware; they are data aware. So no matter how much you study – how much data you acquire – don't make the mistakes that computers, machines and even some scientists make. Don't see the world in only black and white, but look for the grey. Investigate the grey.

And believe in your intuitive experiences. Believe in your perception of images and symbols. But never believe in your data (even your symbolic data) more than you believe in yourself!

Here is a remarkable story told by my friend Tom, which occurred many years ago while he was simply taking a walk:

> As I was looking lovingly at a house that I knew had been for sale, I heard my inner voice clearly saying, 'This house is going to be your house.' Before I could stop myself with thoughts of lack and no funds to make it happen, the voice said, 'You won't know unless you try.'
>
> So I made an appointment with the owner and offered a $6,000 down payment – for which I had not one cent! I also set a date three months from that time for closing. Within weeks I was offered a loan for that exact amount and a gift of $5,000 from another friend to help with the repairs. Starting with nothing but my inner guidance, a sixteen-room house was mine!

Tom's 'real world' data (his cheque book) told him that getting that house was impossible. But his spirit told him to believe (and take action). And when he believed, so did the rest of the world.

* * * * *

10

Choose!

The third important component in the A, B, C's of applied intuition is choose. This step corresponds to the step of *responding* in spontaneous intuition (see Chapter 3). But there is one very significant difference between the two. Responding implies *reaction* whereas choosing indicates *action*. Here are the primary actions of inner choosing:

- Choose your intuition.
- Choose to act on *your* behalf.

In many ways these choices are about the same thing – choosing your highest in everything. Though there are some similarities let's take a look at each individually.

Choose Your Intuition

Since choosing is action, this statement can be read as: 'Act upon your inner guidance.' If you feel you're being guided to take a certain course of action (and you *know* that it's in your best interest, in spite of the difficulties it might impose), then go for it. And don't linger. Consider the rabbit in the woods. He can even get away from the wily fox if his instincts are sharp and he responds to them quickly enough.

I have a friend, a writer for a very popular television show, who didn't choose to listen to her intuition about ending a difficult marriage. She says she had to 'bury' her intuition just to keep the marriage going. This is dangerous because when you bury your intuition in one part of your life, it's harder to know it in the rest of your life. Though she doesn't regret taking the time that she needed, she finally listened. She now says her life 'from that moment on has become richer by the day'.

Choosing your intuition is the same as choosing your truth; but there are times when the message seems unclear, you're not sure it's right, or you just don't feel ready. Even if you hesitate because of fear of change, that, too, is reflective of some part of your emotional truth. Seek to understand where the conflict lies. Is there a payoff in hesitating? To what extent are your fears influencing your action or non-action? Take some time to consider all these factors. Meditate on the message and seek further guidance. And please, don't add guilt to the existing complex of emotions. Most importantly, be honest with yourself. And know, *know*, that if you are pursuing your deepest understanding in any situation, you are still choosing your spirit!

Practices in Choosing Your Inner Voice

1. *Discover what your intuition is guiding you to do*. Ask every day, 'What does my spirit ask of me today?'

2. *Get out of reactionary behaviour*. If you're always reacting in a kneejerk fashion to events around you, you're not taking the time to consider your choices and the actions they call you to make. Reacting relinquishes your freedom to choose.

3. Try to *be more spontaneous and even fearless in your decision-making*. Understand that acting quickly through choice is not the same as *reacting* immediately without thought. If reacting is your general pattern though, take your time in assessing the situation. Choose action instead of reaction. You can be spontaneous after you have built a new pattern of thinking first and acting later.

4. *Every morning determine one thing you can do for yourself today*, and be sure to do it.

5. *Open yourself to the mind of your spirit* every day through any of the brief exercises shown in this book or through those you design yourself. You don't have to spend a lot of time with these processes – just a couple of moments frequently throughout your day.

6. Make a commitment to *build a practice of meditating several times a week* (daily if you can). It is the best way to integrate your personal mind with your intuitive mind. And it allows you a more permanent awareness of your spirit.

READY, SET, GO!

Making Decisions

PURPOSE: To integrate the intuitive heart and the intuitive mind in making choices. *By combining the information that guides you with the feelings that honour you, you create a complete course of action.*

PREPARATION: Consider an important decision that's been on your mind. It may be best to start with a situation where you need to determine to act or not to act. Some of our most important decisions come in the form of 'do I or don't I?' (Do I change my career or not? Do I go back to school or not? Do I marry or not?) Of course, the issue you're considering doesn't have to be life changing, but it should be significant enough to carry an emotional punch.

STEPS:

1. Relax your body and release all tension from your face, shoulders and back, and all the way down to your toes. Take three deep, cleansing breaths and relax more deeply with every exhalation.

2. Close your eyes and let go of all busy and distracting thoughts.

Let your consciousness go deep inside your heart, deep inside
your inner space of calm, deep inside your spirit.

3. Think of this situation which requires a decision, and consider
   your choices in the simplest terms.

4. Consider your first choice of action and visualise yourself taking
   this specific action. How do feel emotionally when you see
   yourself acting in this manner? Do you feel good about yourself?
   Do you feel happy or concerned? Does your intuition want you to
   take this action?

5. Next, imagine the outcome. Visualise it as a still photograph with
   the action finished and the outcome fully realised. Put yourself
   completely in that picture. Ask your intuitive heart how it feels now
   that you have arrived. You are now living that outcome every day.
   (You are in your new home. You have got the job you pursued. You
   have moved to a new city. Whatever the goal, you are there.) What
   are your emotions as you see yourself in this new position? Excited
   or trapped? Happy or sad? Are you glad you made that choice? Be
   honest with yourself and let yourself *feel* the answer.

6. Next, visualise yourself *not* taking this action. Imagine your life if
   you keep things the same and don't make this choice. How do you
   feel emotionally when you prevent yourself from realising this
   outcome? Do you feel excited or trapped? Happy or sad? Does the
   situation of staying where you are bring you enthusiasm or dread?

7. Which decision (to take action or not) most honours you and your
   truth? Which decision makes you feel safe? Which decision leads
   to your growth? Go to the heart of your spirit and answer these
   questions in your *knowing*.

8. Before you close this process, be sure to write how you feel about each
   possible outcome in your journal. Revisit the situation in a few days.
   And, as always, be honest with yourself and *know* what you know!

OBSERVATION: The ability to visualise yourself totally in both
   possible outcomes is essential if you are to arrive at the best
   decision. Put yourself there completely, from your soul right
   down to your shoes. Know what it feels like to be there, and know
   whether that outcome allows you to live with integrity. (Being

able to *see* yourself in the outcome is not the same as attaching to the outcome. One helps you to choose, the other only helps you to worry. See the next chapter for more on attachments.)

THE NEXT STEP: After you've tried this process with the larger choices in your life, you can scale it down and use it for your daily choices. Just take a momentary step into the outcome of the little actions you take during the day. How does it feel to be in the outcome of eating that second dessert? When your co-worker presses you into a confrontation, how do you feel afterwards? Doing this with everyday decisions brings you a higher level of consciousness and a greater commitment to your integrity at every level.

*　*　*　*　*

Choose to Act on Your Behalf

Though this choice would seem to be the most obvious one in our lives, it is often the choice we make the least!

Perhaps we grew up in a troubled home or suffered a trauma in childhood. Or perhaps we were never shown that we had the power and potential to fulfil our dreams. Or maybe we were unpopular in school. Whatever the reason, many adults in this wide world have spent years thinking thoughts that diminish their value and self-esteem. For decades they have been committed to destructive behaviour patterns which not only prevent them from *acting* on their own behalf, but also cloud their ability to *recognise* what 'their behalf' would be!

The process of changing thought-forms and behaviour patterns that have been reinforced over many years requires a significant commitment of consciousness and effort. For most of us, the thinking patterns in our brains have been running like wild horses, at their will. Some of them have stampeded all over our well-being, smashing us into states of inertia and joylessness. It is only when we become more conscious of these

BREAK THROUGH

Perhaps there's a dream you'd like to make real or a change you'd like to make in your life, but you've been feeling blocked in your attempt to change – literally blocked. Then suddenly, there before you stands a wall, high and thick, made of stone or brick. Your dreams are on the other side of this wall. You start to become frustrated. You've seen this wall before – almost every day. But now you realise that *you* built this wall! Brick by brick, stone by stone – each brick an unloving thought, each stone a hurtful or sabotaging action. Yet just as you built this wall with each negative thought, statement and action, you can dismantle it by removing them all and changing them to something loving and constructive. And over time, by continuing to choose to act on your own behalf, you will discover that the wall comes down – one day at a time, brick by brick. Determine now what you must remove from your present daily emotional patterns, beliefs and behaviours to stop blocking yourself. Look at the new bricks that you create. Each brick is one little thought, one little step, that you can repeat over and over again each day to build a road to your dreams. Make a list now of the new thoughts and actions that you will use to build your joy every day.

patterns that we can begin to involve the perspective of the unlimited spirit within. You can choose to stop living in old patterns. You can choose to stop denying your potential. To create the life you want, back it up with action: Choose to build the consciousness of your spirit.

The only way to build this level of consciousness is through the discipline of practising new thoughts, affirmations and self-honouring actions. Now, don't run from this because I used the word discipline. Its meaning has become rather twisted over the years, so it might be helpful to take a second look at it.

The root words for discipline and disciple come from Latin: *disciplina* means 'learning' and *discipulus* means 'one who learns'. The first definition of discipline is 'a branch of knowledge or learning', but its secondary meaning, 'training that develops self-control', has now become the most accepted. Indeed, for most people 'discipline' is now associated with punishment rather than training. It's no wonder we shudder and strain under the weight of this 'dreadful' word that connotes only hard work. Still, we must recognise the difference discipline can make in our lives.

In any endeavour, any purpose, you must take the action of that purpose. Nothing will ever happen if you just think about it! *Becoming anything requires repetition of action. Repetition of action requires discipline, the learning of new behaviours.*

Discipline is your partner in becoming. It is the action that manifests what you want in your life. Exercise and good nutrition will bring you physical well-being. Study can open new interests and careers. A few minutes of focusing inwardly on your intuitive mind every day can give you the universe. And loving thoughts and self-honouring actions will create a life of wonderment and joy. Discipline is a gift you give to yourself! So, let me say it again – just a little louder this time:

Discipline
is your partner in
becoming!

* * * * *

Embrace it.
And redefine yourself
as a disciple,
one who learns
a new way!

Choices You Can Make on Your Own Behalf

- *Choose* to notice where your intuition guides you every day. Then choose to take that action even if you've said 'no' before.
- *Choose* only the thoughts that help you believe in yourself and in your intuitive abilities.
- *Choose* to investigate and discover your deepest truth in every situation and relationship in your life.
- *Choose* to honour your truth by doing only what honours and respects you.
- *Choose* to let go of the activities, people, places and thoughts that are toxic, heavy and dark.
- *Choose* the activities, ideas, people and places that make your heart sing.
- *Choose* your spirit in every moment of every day. Whether you are making a movie or making a bed, writing a book or writing a note to the teacher, being a president or a cleaner. Choose to be who you have been forever!

So, stop making excuses for not having the life you want, for living a life denying your truth. To choose the life you want, back it up with action. You have the choice to act on your own behalf! It is your choice. It is always – in every single moment of every single day – your choice.

*   *   *   *   *

11

Detach

Now that you've stayed conscious of your intuitive input and have acted upon it with purpose and intention, what more can be done? That answer brings us to step four: detach.

Detaching seems like something simple, a mere afterthought that can be waved away after all the hard work has been done. But in truth it may be the most challenging step of all, because the act of detaching is not something we do easily. Unlike rats in a maze who will stop running in circles when the cheese is taken away, we humans will run in circles indefinitely even when the result we seek is gone. (This is especially true in romantic relationships when we may be so obsessed with getting 'the cheese' we don't have a clue that the cheese has spoiled!)

There are three ways to detach that can have great impact upon your intuition and your life:

- Detach from any performance anxiety you might have about your intuitive success.

- Detach from the outcome once you have chosen to do what your intuition directs.

- Detach from the personal perspective (the little self) in order to discover your higher reality.

Detach From Performance Anxiety

Performance anxiety often goes hand in hand with any new activity. It's natural, when you are challenging yourself with new tasks, to ask, 'Am I doing this right? Will I get the results I want?'

Learning to work with the intuitive mind triggers these types of doubts even more strongly since it is such a nebulous and intangible experience. But *trust and doubt are mutually exclusive events,* and trust is required for intuition. The bottom line:

> *Worrying about your success*
> *will prevent your success.*

There are three reasons for this. First, if your mind is occupied with second-guessing, then it won't be open to perceiving your intuition. And, second, even when you do receive guidance, your doubts ('Did I get that right?') can prevent you from acting on it. Finally, if you engage in performance anxiety about your intuition, you can't build a regular habit of trust – in your intuition, in yourself or in your choices.

So stay in the flow during any intuitive experience. Don't fill your mind with worry about whether you're doing well, just open your mind. Be aware of those thoughts that question your performance. *I can't do this. What if I'm interpreting the symbol wrong? What if I act on this guidance and I don't succeed?* This kind of thinking is a strong indication that you are worried about the success or failure of your intuitive experience.

Of course, none of these feelings is invalid. Acknowledging your feelings is a must if you are to live with a sense of well-being. Recognise if you are afraid, but recognise, too, that *fear belongs to your personal, temporal self. Strength and invulnerability belong to your spirit.* Any desire you have to hold yourself back may be one of the many bricks in that wall you have constructed to block yourself in your past. Always open yourself to a new perspective through trust.

Detach From the Outcome

In the 'real' world the *end result* has become the gold standard of self-worth. In human history, people's dreams and goals have rarely been about *who* they are; more often they are about *what* they are – what they own, whom they know and whom they can influence.

There is nothing wrong with having dreams about financial and personal success, about improving your life. But the ultimate improvement for any individual is the experience of the true joy of living on your purpose and knowing your spirit every day. In the *real* real world, every physical acquisition, financial position and experience of fame or power is as fleeting and temporary as your first car, the toy your mother didn't get you when you were twelve, or the scoop of ice cream that once fell off your cone into the dirt.

Still, letting go of the end result after an important course of action can be very challenging, regardless of whether that action was directed by your intuition or not. It is a natural thing to hope for beneficial results when you've invested your effort, creativity and time. After all, when you invest your money in stock or a business venture, you would naturally expect a return on that investment.

So what's the problem with wanting good results? *The problem comes not when you act to meet a desired goal, but when your attachment to that outcome is so absolute that your happiness is determined by its success or failure.* If your experience of happiness is determined by an event, you will never recognise *yourself* as the first and greatest source of joy in your life. And you will give your power and your happiness over to events and people outside of your control.

Attachment to Results Can Block Intuition

Attachment to outcome creates feelings of urgency. A sense of urgency may blur the line between what your intuition directs and what drives you through your lower emotions. Your intuition will always put you on the right path to your goals and dreams, but if you have a great sense of urgency about the outcome of this path, then you may also be hearing from another internal voice. In order to be sure, take a step back and weigh all of the information (psychological, logical, financial, emotional, physical, professional and intuitive). Make those decisions that honour you, your life, and your spirit – those that take you to the highest good you can know. If you use this as your guidepost, you'll never go wrong.

Attachment to one outcome inhibits the possibility of other outcomes. Actions may have different results than what you expected (or may ever have imagined). If you look only in one direction for a predetermined outcome, you are not giving unforseen possibilities a chance. If you detach from the outcome you *think* you want, you'll be free to recognise another one that might be better!

Attachment to outcome diminishes the value of the process and the purpose. Many people say, 'If I don't care about the outcome, why should I bother making the effort or doing the work?' They think that not caring how something turns out prevents them from pursuing that goal. It may seem contradictory, but *diminishing the importance of the outcome actually helps you increase the importance of the process*. It gives you a chance to discover a greater passion for each step along the way – to know a greater desire to 'do the work for the work's sake'.

> *Nothing of greatness in the world is ever accomplished without passion.*

For competitors in the Olympic Games it is the passion for their sport. For the author, it is a passion for writing. For the actor it is a passion for acting. Medals, book sales and awards can result from pursuing these passions, but it is still the *passion for the purpose* that is the driving force. So seek to discover where your passions lie. Is there *any* activity that you love with all your heart, can't wait to try or feel compelled to do? If you don't have an answer to that question right away, give it some thought. Consider your past and what you loved as a child. Maybe it's something you thought impossible, an idea you put away a long time ago. If the answer doesn't lie there, then think about what interests you, what makes you curious. If you really looked into these interests, might you grow to love them?

Find your passion!
It is the portal to your purpose.
When you're passionate about your purpose,
that purpose is the outcome!

Steps in Detaching From the Outcome

1. Determine to stay open to all possible outcomes, including those you might think are negative. They could be opportunities in disguise.

2. Reaffirm your trust by surrendering your expectations. Your spirit knows where it's taking you, so go there with curiosity and wonderment.

3. Affirm your belief that the highest good – no matter what – shall happen.

4. Realise that *any* outcome in the physical world is merely one step in the process for your spirit.

In the competitive and race-like conditions of your work, your projects and your life, consider the freedom you can acquire when you realise:

THERE IS NO FINISH LINE!

Detach from the Personal Perspective to Embrace the Spirit!

Our birth is but a sleep and a forgetting:
The Soul that rises with us, our life's Star,
Hath had elsewhere its setting,
And cometh from afar ...

– William Wordsworth

In 'Intimation of Immortality' Wordsworth spoke of how the soul can be forgotten in the physical world. Sadly, his is an example of life imitating art. So much had he changed from the gentle-hearted supporter of the underdog to an arrogant, insufferable and rigid old man that he became one of the most ridiculed poets and parodied men of his time. Ironically, the most popular parody during that time reflected the very duality shown in Wordsworth's poem, often referring to his 'two voices' (one the deep visionary, the other the half-witted didactic). In spite of his early words appreciating the soul, Wordsworth's later behaviour strongly illustrated to his contemporaries the ease with which the personal self *can* forget its eternal reality, the spirit.

We cannot know the intuitive mind fully unless we *remember that spirit is who we are* – indeed, who we always have been in every moment. While that may seem to be an obvious conclusion, it is not so easy when it comes to acting on it. Making the effort to remember our spirit provides a greater perspective and more creative and powerful choices. It allows us to give that spirit a voice in our physical, personal lives.

Yet if you want to be able to have a *dialogue* with that voice, if you want to be able to build a *conscious rapport* with your inner guidance, it will take more than just remembering the spirit. You will need to recall it, restore it to your definition of self, and re-establish it not just in your consciousness but in your actual experience.

How do you experience the spirit when you rely so heavily on the five physical senses to perceive your reality? Well, to put a different spin on a contemporary saying, you quite literally have to:

Get OVER your self!

The metaphor 'Get over your self' usually means to wake up and get out of your ego (and that, indeed, is a very good thing to do if you want to embrace your spirit better), but in this case I mean it quite literally. You have to get *over* or *above* your personal, temporal self. Lift yourself up in your perspective and even in your experience. If you know yourself as something larger than your physical reality, you are not restricted to only the measure of what that physicality can do.

Happily, you don't have to die to get to your spirit, but you do have to put yourself into the higher dimensions from where that spirit comes. The spatial, three-dimensional experience of the physical is limited when compared with the multi-dimensionality of your spirit. Your spirit is not restricted to just one world. Its natural home is a world of grace, light and divine company. It is a home without place or time, a home of several, varied dimensions, and a vast experience of mind, energy and love.

The physical expression of the self, the personality, is a considerably diminutive one, comparatively speaking. Humanity, as broad reaching and profoundly creative as it might seem to be, can measure itself only in terms of the measurable, physical world.

The physical world is just the shallow water where your spirit sticks its toe!

To live in the shallow waters of this three-dimensional world, we have thrown our waking consciousness into the smallest part of what we are. The more we are restricted to that limited world, the more we forget the rest of our body (our spirit, our joy and our real power) – until, finally, all that we are in belief and in experience is nothing more than the tiny, negligible 'toe'. The vantage point from this lesser, physical perspective must, indeed, be inconsequential compared with a reality that sets its clock by eternity and makes its home in heaven. And we must begin now to make this clock and this home our own.

One individual who (like too many others) has discovered the most extreme type of restriction known in the physical world is Christopher Reeve. Since his C2 spinal cord injury during a riding accident in May 1995, he has known every aspect of despair and every grasp at hope that any individual could. 'I began to think: Whether or not there is a God is not so important. Spirituality itself, the belief that there is something greater than ourselves, is enough.'

'I think,' he continues in his book *Still Me* (published by Random House), 'the old adage "God is love" is literally true, whether or not you actually believe in God. Thinking that way helped me get past the "me-me-me" – my body, my problems, my condition, myself … I gradually stopped wondering, What life do I have? and began to consider, What life can I build?'

There are so many ways of being trapped in this world. Battered women are trapped by their husbands. Drug addicts are trapped by their drugs. Abused children are trapped by their parents. Even Princess Diana was trapped by her celebrity.

Yet of all the ways to feel trapped in this tiny little 'toe' we call a body, I can't imagine anything that could induce a greater feeling of defencelessness than paralysis. From the constant dependency upon others to the endless moments when an oxygen tube would 'pop off', leaving Christopher praying that someone would respond to the alarm so that he could breathe again – every situation was just another indication of his powerlessness. But Christopher believed in 'something greater'. It was something that led him out of the 'me' that was trapped. And it was his belief in what he could be (not what he had lost) that moved him from powerlessness to power and from immobility to action.

> ### *BREAK THROUGH*
>
> Close your eyes and take a deep breath. Imagine
> for a moment that you are no longer your body. It
> is not a part of who you are. You are thought. You
> are will. You are power. How deep does this power
> go inside you? How far does this presence extend
> around you? Take another deep breath and *know*
> the body of energy you are.

Through the belief in ourselves as larger beings, we can take
larger action in our lives. But to have a greater connection to
the mind or our spirits, we have to know ourselves in that mind
and from that perspective. How do we reacquaint ourselves with
the giants we really are? We have to un-become the 'toe' and
awaken to the consciousness, the viewpoint, of the giant. Though
this will happen naturally in death, we can do this *now* through
practice.

The following brief process takes only a few moments. So
before you read any further, give yourself a peek into the larger
world of your spirit and do this exercise now.

READY, SET, GO!

Lifting Yourself to Your Greater Reality

PURPOSE: To detach yourself from a narrow, physical world perspective by lifting yourself to the higher perspective of your spirit.

PREPARATION: Choose a space and time when you can relax and go
deep within. Open yourself to 'see' through your imagery.

STEPS:

1. Close your eyes and take three deep breaths as you let go of your cares and worries of the day.

2. Use your imagination to see your self rising up through the top of your head and into the vastness that is your spirit. With each inhalation feel yourself getting bigger and bigger (expanding your chest as you inhale helps you know the feeling of largeness).

3. Imagine that you grow to be as big as the giant in *Jack and the Beanstalk*. As your head begins to lift higher and higher – first through the ceiling, then through the trees, then into the clouds – begin to look down at the things and the people below as they grow smaller and smaller.

4. Don't make any judgements or mental assessments of the situation; simply give yourself complete permission to 'see' in your *imagination* the new and growing perspective that moving into your larger reality allows.

5. Take another deep breath. In your imaging, really *become* this giant.

6. 'Look down' upon all the animated activity in the smaller world below you. And while you do, take a glance at your smaller, personal self. Are there any narrow perspectives impeding that little self about which you can now see a wider view?

7. Continue to look at the rest of the smaller world. What else do you notice that might bring you insight about the people and events in the little world below?

OBSERVATION: This process takes you to a broader experience of your intuitive mind and the great vision of your spirit. It helps you become more fluent in the practice of imaging and requires you to suspend your linear and analytical mind. It enhances spontaneous perception and furthers your ability to trust your images and symbols. Consequently, you have not only lifted yourself above the personal world to the greater view of your spirit, but you have practised the devices that will make that perspective real every day.

THE NEXT STEP: Now that you have taken a brief excursion to find
the vision of your spirit, commit to taking this new, larger
perspective into your daily life. Do this process when you're angry
and when you're trapped in a narrow perspective or attached to
an outcome. Practise giving yourself a glimpse of this new
vantage point regularly. It is a vantage point that allows you more
freedom than you have ever known in the 'little' world.

*   *   *   *   *

12

Experiment!

*No matter what activity
or practice we are pursuing,
there isn't anything that isn't made easier
through constant familiarity and training.
Through training, we can change;
we can transform ourselves.*

– The Dalai Lama

Now we come to the last step in our A,B,C's of intuition, **A**sk, **B**elieve, **C**hoose, **D**etach, **E**xperiment. Each component is as necessary as any other in developing an ongoing relationship with your spirit. Some of these steps are more difficult than others, requiring constant practice until your new discipline (or area of study) unfolds. Others demand great honesty and even painful inner searching to loosen the shackles of old habits and defeating thought patterns. Some steps require you to stay light on your feet, ready at any time of the day to step across a threshold of discovery. And some challenge you in all of these ways.

This last step is perhaps my favourite: Experiment! To me *it is the playground of discovery.* Your spirit is your playmate and your best friend. And, happiest of all, the playground is always open! Now, don't misunderstand me. Just because I call this step the playground, doesn't mean that it's optional! Experimenting and practising (or training as the Dalai Lama called it) are absolutely necessary to bring your fullest experience to *any* area of development. In order to learn new sports, you have to train your muscles in a new way. If you want to play a musical instrument beautifully, you have to practise it. If you want to learn a new language, you have to speak it. And in order to talk to your intuition, you have train yourself to reach inside. This can only happen with practice – *regular and frequent practice*.

So, if it's practice that's required, why isn't this step called *exercise* instead of experiment? First, investigating the inner mind is a little like the early scientists investigating the unknown. Often you're not sure exactly what to expect, but you know that if you keep looking and experimenting with different models, discovery will be yours. Second, every person is different in the experience of intuition. Some are more inclined to feeling, some to seeing, some to sensing, and so on. You need to experiment with lots of different models to truly discover your own methods. (And you need to keep experimenting, no matter how far you have developed, because the techniques that work for you may keep growing and changing over time.) Finally, experimenting gives you the chance to live every day with a sense of curiosity. So keep trying new methods. Use those you find in this book, or change them to make them your own. Design some new processes for yourself. However you do it, just be sure to experiment – every day, many times a day. If you live on the threshold of discovery, if you seek your spirit with the passion of Madame Curie and the persistence of Thomas Edison, you cannot fail!

Clinical Experiments

Speaking of scientists, let's take a look at clinical 'psi' tests and experiments. Psi is the general term encompassing all phenomena in the field of parapsychology, including intuition, ESP, telepathy (mental communication with another), precognition (knowing future events), and psychokinesis (moving physical objects with the mind). These experiments, of course,

would be performed in a lab, with very specific subject popu-
lations, and under strict protocols of testing techniques and
environmental controls (right down to the temperature of the
room). My academic work in psychology brought me a little
closer to these types of experiments than, perhaps, I might
have wished. My graduating thesis was 'The Experimental
Design for Testing the Occurrence of Psi and ESP in Fraternal
and Identical Twins'. If you think the title seems dry, you
should've been there for the testing! (By the way, the identical
twins scored higher.)

Almost everybody knows a little bit about these types of
experiments, even if only from watching them in the movies.
You've seen the cards with the wavy lines, circles, stars, etc.
and the individual subjects divided by partitions, one looking
at the cards and the other 'receiving' the information. Such is
the nature of clinical testing. It requires dozens of subjects per-
forming hundreds of runs, with each run comprising hundreds
of trials. Each trial is determined a 'hit' or 'miss', and each hit
or miss has to be recorded and tallied to determine the statisti-
cal significance of probability. (Heaven help us!)

What does all of this have to do with intuition? Some
important conclusions have been made by a few notables in
the clinical arena. J.B. Rhine and his colleagues at Duke
University (including J.G. Pratt and Louisa Rhine) set the bar
for parapsychological research in the early twentieth century,
and there is a great deal to be learned by their decades of
work and the clinical studies they have published over the
years.

The experiments that I find most telling are those determining the effects of test conditions on performance. The test
conditions that most increased performance were novelty of
the material, the possibility of reward, and the presence of
competition.

What can these tests tell you about your own experiments? First, keep them fresh and new. The novelty and
diversity of your intuitive processes will keep your interest

level (and consequently your perception level) high. One of the reasons I have included so many different exercises in this book is to try to diminish boredom. (In the lab, with continuous exposure to one task, ESP subjects did not develop greater skills but actually got bored and declined in performance.) So don't get in a rut! Even if there are certain exercises or types of exercises that you really enjoy doing, change them and shift them around a bit. Keep your experiments novel, and mould them to fit your personal quest.

The next component that increased perception is the possibility of reward – in other words, the value you receive for making the effort! So find the value in each intuitive process as well as in the discovery that it brings to you.

The third factor increasing success was the presence of competition during the experiment. I'm not suggesting that you set up your intuitive work as a contest with others, but it may be a very good thing to discuss your investigations with someone close to you who shares your interest. The level of emotional and intuitive discovery can certainly be elevated through your conversations with others.

Each of these factors contributes a very important component: the presence of emotional content. Subjects cared more about the exercise when they weren't bored. They had more feelings about the mundane task when there was a reward connected to it. They had higher emotional experience when they were in a contest. (My favourite contest took place when the divinity students at Duke challenged a group of gamblers being tested in the lab. Both groups scored significantly higher than chance – a considerable four times higher. But neither group could beat the other. Their scores were almost identical![13])

So, how you feel counts! *Your intuitive perceptions will be more significant if what you investigate matters.* Emotional content is an important part of the intuitive experience.

You will find dozens of books about developing your intuition that ask you to decide who's on the phone before you answer, pick which lift will stop on your floor, guess how many emails you have today, or decide the winners of football games and horse races. I call these 'finger exercises', much like the scales a musician might practise on the guitar or piano. These may give you some practice, but it is best to do exercises that carry a purpose. After all, the emotional experience of listening to musical scales is certainly not the same as enjoying a symphony.

These little 'who's on the phone' exercises may be fun and may help you flex your intuitive muscles, but you will still be dealing with the same factors that influenced Rhine's subjects in his lab. Intuitive 'finger exercises' are like the cards with the wavy lines. They provide a means of practising, but they're not going to do much to enhance your life! Nor will guessing the colour of your boss's tie help you to develop a greater intuitive repertoire. Here's why:

A need to know increases intuitive receptivity.

Though the purpose of listening to our intuition is 'to get answers in our lives', accuracy is not the result we're seeking. The need for accuracy (or, as we've seen before, the need for a particular outcome) can, in fact, get in the way. And with intuitive finger exercises, the need for accuracy can be downright sabotaging.

To have the highest experience of intuitive perception, you must care in some way about some part of the process. Because you are unlikely to have strong feelings about which lift comes first, the only thing left to care about will be whether you're right or wrong! If you do finger exercises frequently (intuiting your phone calls, the exact time, number of emails, etc.), you will reinforce your attachment to being right or wrong which will increase your performance anxiety. And if, heaven forbid, you are unsuccessful in your perception of these outcomes, you will increase your self-doubts, undermine your further success and reinforce the belief that you're *not* intuitive.

So why not learn a little something from all that research at Duke University: Make what's really important *important!* If you're going to spend even a few seconds on an intuitive exercise while waiting for a lift, spend it in discovery! If you want to use your environment to get in touch with your intuition, just ask, 'What do I see around me that reflects something I can learn about myself?' Then look for it. Now, that's quality time!

This chapter, then, is devoted exclusively to the experiments you can practise. There are three sections, each representing a different area of your life: work, relationships, and the journey of your own self-discovery. Do any experiment you wish, any number of times you wish. There are no right or wrong ways to do these experiments. Just remember to trust, trust, trust!

Intuition in Business

Choose a Professional

If you need the services of a broker, lawyer, accountant or some other professional, follow these steps. First, investigate the candidates thoroughly. Consider their references, history and experience. See if you can arrive at a viable choice through investigation. If not, do the following process:

Close your eyes and imagine that you have put *everything* of value in your life – your house, your savings, your car, your family, even your health – into a velvet pouch. Everything that you care about is in this sack that you are now holding. Now picture the two or three professionals on your short list. Imagine them standing before you. To which professional would you give all your valuables? Whom would you trust with your life? Notice every feeling – even the slightest hesitation or a sigh of relief – as you imagine yourself handing the pouch to each person respectively. Do this process again later until you feel confident with your choice.

BREAK THROUGH

Close your eyes and imagine your job is a liquid –
pouring out of a tap and into a large sink in front
of you. After you've put the plug in, the sink
begins to fill up with the liquid that is your job.
What does it look like? How does it make you
feel? Now it's time to get your hands into your
job. Submerge them into the liquid and let it
cover your hands completely. As you get deeper
and deeper into your job, the liquid even covers
your arms. What colour and consistency is the
liquid? What do your hands look like as you lift
them up, dripping over the sink? How do you
feel? Are you excited about 'handling' this liquid
and this colour? Or do you want to wash your
hands clean? What does this experience tell you
about your work and your purpose in it?

Make a Mission Statement

Think about your purpose at work and the purpose your spirit
holds for your life. Even if you're not exactly sure what that is,
consider the things that interest you and that you've enjoyed
most. Where do your job and your life's purpose meet? How can
you integrate them? If they don't exactly connect, what elements
of your life's truth can you bring to your work? Create a very
clear, very simple statement – just one or two sentences – that
describes your highest intention at work. Memorise it and refer
to it frequently. Every time you have a task or a project that
seems to contradict that intention, ask your intuition how you
can bring a higher truth to that task. See if you can find the
greatness in the little things you do.

Your Intuitive Financial Planner

If your broker or financial advisor has given you some investments to consider, try this process. First, make a list of the names of each recommended stock or mutual fund. Then go through the list slowly, holding each name in your consciousness one at a time. Close your eyes, take a deep breath and imagine your left hand outstretched with your palm up. As you hold one name in your mind, imagine a stack of coins placed in your left hand. How many are there? How heavy are they? Do this with each investment and notice the weight or number of coins you gather with each. Notice the difference between each stack.

Help! Get Me Out of This Job!

If you are in a job that you no longer find appropriate to your truth, these steps will help you get back on the right track:

1. Think about when you first noticed a distaste for this job or this type of work. What specifically about the job began to challenge your sense of well-being? What have been the payoffs for staying in the job?

2. Make a complete list of *everything* you hate about your job – from mundane tasks to the feelings of lack that it evokes in you (lack of creativity, lack of appreciation, for example). Are you willing to continue living with these sacrifices on a daily basis?

3. If you decide that it's time to look for another job, or perhaps another career, make a list of all the activities you love and those you find the most interesting and exciting. Look deep inside and ask your intuition for every joyful option. (Later you might want to consider creating your own business. Even if it might take a few years, think about what you can do now to plant the seeds for this opportunity.)

4. Compare the details of jobs you see advertised with the items on both your lists. Eliminate every job that would require you to do anything on your 'hate' list. (You can't

live with integrity if you spend 40 hours a week doing something you hate. Don't even consider it!)

5. Eliminate any job that wouldn't give you a sense of purpose and fulfilment, anything that wouldn't give your spirit a voice in your life.

6. After you have eliminated the jobs that you don't want, eliminate those that would conflict with other goals. (For instance, if you're a new mother and you want to nurse your baby, you couldn't also be a stewardess and spend most of your week in the air!)

7. Once you have narrowed the field, compare the remaining job descriptions with the list of things you love to do. Which comes closest to that list? Ask your intuition to show you the job that you will love to live with every day!

Intuition in Relationships

Reading Other People

Knowing the way other people feel and think can bring great insight – whether you're dealing with a romantic relationship, going to an important business meeting or just wanting to be sensitive to family and friends. You've probably been advised at some point to put yourself in someone else's place, but usually this just means trying to see this person's point of view. Here's a new way to try it – with your inner senses.

Take a moment now to think of a person whom you would like to understand better. Picture this person as if he were standing right in front of you. Close your eyes, take a deep breath and picture yourself stepping right into that person. Become that person and notice how your body feels. Is it tense or loose, strong or weak? Go deep, and use the first-person 'I' to describe everything. Go to your heart – what emotions do you feel as this person? Take a look down at your clothes. Why did you wear those clothes today? As this other person, ask yourself the following questions, and trust completely the first thing you perceive. *What do I want in my relationship? What do I need? What are the obstacles in my life? What do I see in my future?*

Stay inside the first-person perspective while asking each of these questions. And stay out of your own head. Remember that you're doing this process to gain greater insight. Allow yourself to ask any other questions that will lead to more understanding. When you've finished, take a few minutes to note your observations in your journal.

Dealing with Problem People

Quick, think of a person who causes difficulties for you at work or in your personal life. Close your eyes and image that person in your mind. Ask your spirit what is the dynamic inside this person that causes him or her to behave in a hurtful, closed-off or disruptive way (to you and/or to others). *How does this person's behaviour represent his or her own feelings of lack?* What new insight can you discover about this individual's fear and vulnerability? Does knowing this person's fear give you a new perspective? Ask your intuition now for a *new approach* in dealing with this person, one that will build a greater sense of peace for both of you.

Radar Your Teachers

Take a quick scan of your day yesterday and make a mental list of all the people who were your teachers. Remember, people teach by example (good and bad), and sometimes by provoking you to discover some truth about yourself. Of all the teachers in your life yesterday, which one evoked the strongest response? Is there a lesson you can identify in that response? Are you grateful for the opportunity to learn it? Tomorrow, ask your intuition to spotlight your teachers for you – even before their lessons begin. Look for them with an open heart wherever you go.

Intuition in Self-Discovery

BREAK THROUGH

Envision that a certain problem is a suit of clothes, and put it on. What is it made of? How does it feel? What colour (or colours) is it? Close your eyes and notice how much of you (and which parts of your body) these clothes cover. How much of your life and your self-definition have you wrapped up in this problem? What do you need to do now to change the fabric or shape of this suit of clothes? Can you shed it altogether?

Look Into Your Future

In this exercise you are not meant to focus on accuracy or attach to the outcome of your intuitive predictions. Your spirit lives in an eternal world unrestricted by our calendars. To glimpse into the future or the past, you will need to engage your timeless spirit mind. Once or twice a week, close your eyes and ask your intuition for a few symbolic 'predictions' for the coming week. Remember, this is about your daily life; keep it simple. Ask for just three insights – a few words or short phrases about what's coming to your personal life in the immediate future. Don't look for large events; you're not Nostradamus! Just note a single symbol for each prediction in your journal or in a separate notebook that you keep for intuitive exercises. Record each insight on its own line, leaving space for the result, if any.

For instance, one day you may note the following three symbols: a heart, a surprise at work, water. When you look back at that entry a week later, you may find that you had a loving message from a friend on Tuesday, a new computer at work on Friday, and a broken pipe in the basement on Saturday. Or you may have experienced only the last two, but a month later you might get a call from a friend telling you that you were on her mind that specific week.

Remember, there is no such thing as 'hits' and 'misses'. You can never have an inaccurate symbol – only an inaccurate interpretation. The symbol's meaning, or what it represents, may only require time to give you an understanding of it.

Another form of this exercise is to go mentally to a distant place or future time. Using all your senses, write a brief description of the sights, sounds, smells and feelings you experience in your journal. Do this occasionally to broaden your experience of all times and places.

Live Your Dreams

Are you really in the habit of acting on your own behalf? Here is a process to help you find out.

1. On a small piece of paper write the top three goals you would like to accomplish in five years. Which dreams would you like to have made real five years from now?

2. On a second sheet of paper, list the top three goals you wish to achieve by next year. (They can be from the first list, or they can be different goals.)

3. On a third piece of paper note the top five items on your List of Things To Do this week. They don't have to be urgent; they just have to be what you intend to do. Even 'clearing out the kitchen cupboards' or 'paying the bills' will do.

4. Now take a look at all your lists. Does any item on this week's list represent an action required for one of your five-year or one-year goals? If so, is it an action which you pursue frequently, with great passion and effort?

5. Of course, there may be *no* item on this week's list which would lead to one of your five-year goals. (You would be surprised at how this is true for most people. When I

teach this process, there is rarely even 30 per cent of the class who are taking action this week to meet their five-year or even one-year goals.) If you have a goal to become more physically fit, but you rarely exercise or pursue the sports that would help you get fit, you have effectively chosen to maintain your present level of fitness. The same is true for any of your dreams.

6. Choice and action are utterly inseparable. The action you take in any situation is the absolute physical expression of your true choice. *If you have decided upon a list of five-year goals which would change your life's experience but you haven't changed today's activities, then the real goal that you have chosen is to stay exactly as you are.* So if you want to live your dreams in five years or next year or next month, you have to *live your dreams today*. And that means 'choose those actions today'!

Power Generator

Do this exercise whenever you need to tap into your power and carry it with you through the world – for strength and confidence, for business meetings, for maintaining your intention when you know it might be challenged and, especially, for remembering who you are and where you live.

Take a slow, easy breath, and with the exhalation release everything that is on your mind. As you continue to take deep, slow breaths, begin to straighten your spine from the waist up, one vertebra at a time. Do this slowly and notice your posture changing. When you reach the top of your spine, push your shoulders back and feel your chest open along with your heart centre (the energy centre at the middle of your chest just to the right of the heart). Affirm your openness to receive and to share.

Now, you begin to feel a beautiful ball of light deep in your chest at your heart centre. It's almost as if the hand of God reached into the middle of your back, opened up, and there, resting in its palm is the brilliant seed of power that began the universe! And now that power is in you! Its light begins to grow, filling you up – to the top of your head and down to your toes. Feel its warmth and power. Soon it begins radiating out from you. This absolute creative energy and wisdom will precede you, fill you and follow you throughout your day.

You will stand taller, feel stronger, and be more compassionate. And though others can't see it, everyone you meet will feel it and recognise it in some way. And you will recognise this potential in them – even if they don't recognise it in themselves. You can make the world different with this creative light and power. And the only moment you will stop feeling it is when – through thought or deed – you divide yourself from it. If you find yourself doing this, all you have to do is reconnect. Straighten your back, look inside, and tap the power that is available to you always.

*　*　*　*　*

Personal Study for Part III

1. Think about the ways you perceive your intuitive insights
   – through images, ideas, words and feelings. Take a few
   minutes each day for a week to practise seeing, hearing,
   sensing, and knowing. Don't look for any information;
   just look for the experience. Write briefly about it in your
   journal.

2. Consider the doubts that have passed through your mind
   in the last few days. You might have to think hard about
   this because doubtful moments can be subtle. Did those
   doubts cause you to hold yourself back in any way?
   Create just one statement that you can use to release
   doubt and replace it with a higher truth about yourself.
   For instance, 'I release doubt and I believe in my ability to
   _____ (name the purpose here).' Or 'I trust that
   this path is leading me to an opportunity I can yet
   discover.' Remember to use the statement every time a
   doubt enters your mind.

3. Make an observation in your journal about how you
   checked in for your intuitive messages today. What was
   the most important message you received? What can you
   learn from it?

4. Plan to chronicle your day tomorrow not by the passage
   of time but by your opportunities to choose. Stay alert for
   the choices that you can make on your own behalf. *Do not
   let the morning, afternoon or evening go by without making
   a choice that honours your sense of truth and purpose.*
   Whether each choice is small or large, congratulate
   yourself for making it. Determine to build this habit of
   higher choice every day.

Part IV

From Blocks to Becoming

The soul knows everything. Nothing new can surprise it. Nothing is greater than it. Let others be afraid, but the soul is not afraid of anything; it lives according to its own laws. It is greater than space and older than time. It gives us courage against all the misfortunes of life.

— Ralph Waldo Emerson

13

Blocked and Blue

Overcoming Obstacles in Your Intuition

As with any new endeavour, there are always questions about every aspect of the experience. This is true with intuition as well. In this chapter, we'll take a look at the most often asked questions and concerns that people face when they begin to open to their intuition. As you continue to open to your higher mind, give yourself permission to face each obstacle or concern without judging yourself. Understand that everything happens in cycles. So be patient and look for your truth everywhere – even in the things that seem to block you.

Frequently Asked Questions

What if my intuition tells me to make a change I don't want to make?
Though it's true that listening to your intuition brings you a greater feeling of well-being, what you 'hear' won't always be what you want to hear. Your intuitive perceptions may sometimes tell you to do something you may not find easy to do.

As a matter of fact, when you begin a full experience of intuitive listening, it will probably cause some things in your life to rupture! The things that you've been denying will become apparent to you, and you will no longer be able to avoid the changes you need to make.

I have a client in New York, an architect, whose intuition and dreams directed her to take a teaching position at a top US university. She was very hesitant because this would involve leaving the city, her friends, job, family and home. She did take up the post though, and found she was able to maintain her relationships in New York *and* have an exciting new career.

Staying open to your perceptions, whether or not the information you're receiving is pleasant or unpleasant, is imperative. Be honest with yourself. Let go of denial. Any denial in your life is a block not only to your intuition but to your joy!

What if I see something that frightens me?

This is a variation on the previous question. Many people are afraid of opening their awareness to the intuitive mind because they're afraid of what they might see. For instance, what if you were to see an image of a divorce, a bad school report, or even a car accident?

There are two important things to remember. First, the future is not set in stone. It is dependent upon your free will. You will create it through your thoughts and actions. It is up to you to design it. Second, your spirit speaks to you with the use of symbols. What you perceive as an image about the future may be a metaphor for your growth rather than a literal event.

Here's an example of just such an occurrence. On one beautiful summer's day many years ago I was teaching a class in Lily Dale, New York, about some of these very topics. Though my sister, Sandy, was otherwise occupied, I talked her into changing her plans so that she could try some of the processes I was to teach that day. I conducted an imagery process which took the participants five years into the future. After the process, it was clear that Sandy was upset. During a break she told me that she had mentally heard a message about death. I immediately looked for answers in my own guidance and told Sandy that her image represented the death of an old way of thinking and the birth of a new sense of purpose and self-actualisation. I felt this truly to be so and reminded her of it often over the following five years. (I had felt very responsible, after all.)

Well, the five-year time period came and went many years ago. Some very important transitions occurred, and even some endings for my sister (but not the one she feared). It was at that very five-year mark that my sister and her husband adopted two children from Russia. Their freewheeling adult lifestyle gave way to new responsibilities and the new, wondrous embrace of a loving family. She also wrote a book about relationships (*Secrets of Attraction*, published by Hay House) which required her to cut back on her counselling time in order to write, lecture and teach.

So you see, these images – even those which might seem difficult – can be metaphors for the opportunities to grow and change, to know yourself better in the truth of your spirit.

BREAK THROUGH

What is your greatest fear in life? Take a moment to close your eyes and imagine it. Really look at it. What does this fear represent about your history? How are you keeping that history alive by keeping the fear alive? Your greatest fear will often point the way to your greatest lesson. If this fear were your classroom, what would you need to do to graduate? How can this fear become an opportunity for you? Keep coming back to this classroom until this fear holds no more power over you.

What if I don't 'see' anything?

'I can't see anything' is a sentiment I hear time and again in my beginners' classes. But the truth is, everyone can 'see' in the mind's eye. All you have to do is practise. Close your eyes and imagine an apple, your favourite chair, a person you know, a picture you love, your kitchen at home – anything and everything – until you become comfortable with the way *you* see.

Some people 'see' in concepts. You may not be able to envision a green apple, but you are certainly able to hold that concept in your mind. Consider what happens when somebody tells you, 'Don't think of a pink elephant.' You can't help but hold that image – visually or conceptually – in your experience!

In truth, difficulty in perceiving images is more about an inability to trust than a lack of imaging skills. But if you find that happening to you, simply insist on an intuitive answer and *open* yourself to the first thing you perceive. Just one little corner of an image or a piece of an idea is all you need to begin a message. Keep practising with the exercises in Part III. Keep releasing your doubts every time they come up, and practise, practise, practise!

BREAK THROUGH

It is when things are most difficult that we most need our intuition. Yet because of the circumstances around us, we may not be able to move beyond the anxiety and noise of confusion.

Think of a real place where you have found great peace, or recall an image from a book, movie or painting that brings tranquillity to your mind. This is your place of trust where you can feel safe. Close your eyes and go there for a few moments now. Take a deep breath and really be there. Practise going there in your mind frequently so that you can bring this peace into any situation at will. Do this for a few moments several times a day. Remind yourself to go to your trust – especially when life gets stormy.

Will I lose my grip on reality? Will I go crazy if I 'listen to voices'?

Some people question their sanity if they 'listen to voices'. While there are some pathological disorders that may involve hearing voices, those voices certainly won't tell you what your intuitive voice would (which is, primarily, to do good for yourself and respect yourself and others).

If you ever notice inner voices that make you feel angry, threatened or jealous, they are probably the voices of fear, victimisation or self-doubt. And they are far more likely to stem from a difficult history or sabotaging behaviour than from insanity.

Carl Jung spoke with (and listened to) his intuitive voice all the time. This visionary and pioneer in psychology was a highly practical and pragmatic researcher who maintained copious records of his research and client observations. Clearly, it is possible to be both logical and intuitive!

Always remember, you have free will and all of your decisions and choices are up to you. You can receive messages about your life from many sources – your intuition, your emotions, your friends, your accountant, your weekly horoscope. And you can choose to follow any or all of them. Freedom of choice is always yours, but choosing to listen to your intuition, the voice of your truth, may be the sanest choice of all.

If I practise becoming more sensitive to my intuition, will I become too sensitive to negative people and situations around me? Will I lose my boundaries?

Becoming more intuitive does not mean you're going to turn into a 'psychic sponge', soaking up all the negativity from everybody you meet. Being more open to your wisdom will help you understand the toxicity in the world around you (and sometimes in you), so that you can take action in your life and your world to help healing take place for all.

What will other people think of me if I make a decision based on a gut feeling without analysis or proof?
For the most part, intuitive experiences are not physical in nature; so you will rarely have physical proof. But lack of concrete evidence doesn't have to be a block. As a matter of fact it can be a boon, because it demands that you put faith in yourself – not in concrete proof or in other people, or even in your analytical assessment.

Your intuition requires you to let go of limiting thoughts. Doubting yourself is a limiting thought, *but over-analysis of your intuition can be very limiting, too.* It limits you to thinking in terms of narrow, physical world constructs. It's true that intuition won't make you crazy, but you do have to be *out of your mind* to experience it! So get out of your mind, get out of your analysis and get out of your need for proof. Enjoy the gift of your intellect but enjoy your intuition, too. Your intuition is about what you feel, not what you think. So *feel* the experience and don't think about proof.

As for others' opinions of you, if intuition is not about what *you* think, it certainly isn't about what *other people* think! Trust yourself and make your own choices.

How can I deal with uncertainty about my intuitive experience?
When people are developing their intuitive skills, uncertainty is their most frequent concern. How can I be sure it's my spirit talking and not my emotions? How can I be sure I'm not making this up? What if I'm only telling myself what I want to hear?

The first, last and best test of whether the voice that's speaking to you is your intuition is this: Does the guidance it gives honour you, allow you to grow, lead you to new self-understanding and, ultimately, take you to a higher experience of your joy? (This joy refers not to immediate gratification but to a greater sense of your purpose.) You can ask this question about any intuitive directive – or, indeed, any course of action – that you might consider in your life.

Just as you can identify individual intuitive messages by the feelings behind them, the real sign that you are building a regular habit of listening to your spirit is how you feel about yourself every day. The activities that spirit directs may not be easy, but you will always feel a greater sense of confidence, self-understanding and purpose when you pursue them. Conversely, if you are consistently unhappy, unfulfilled, and feeling bad about yourself, that is a sign you are not giving your spirit a voice in your life. So begin to listen and to practise. Don't put obstacles in your path by not trusting the information or the source. Trust in your own voice and you will open yourself to your real source of love, compassion and helpfulness.

When you let go of uncertainty, you begin to recognise your spirit's hand in everything. Your spirit can provide help through intuitive messages, by bringing you a teacher, by leading you to an opportunity, or even by helping you find the right book or article. If any experience honours who you are, then you need not question its origin or its name. Your spirit is probably behind it. And, in the end, if you really want to get to know the voice of your spirit, it doesn't matter *what* you call it. It only matters that you do call it.

Here is an exercise that helps to remove uncertainty: Billet Reading. 'Billet' is French for 'a small piece of paper' or 'ticket'. Spiritualists have used billets for over a century to acquire input from the spirit self (or – for mediums – from the spirits of others) without letting personal consciousness get in the way.

If you find yourself questioning your objectivity, here's how billets can help you remove your hopes, fears and doubts from your intuitive investigations.

READY, SET, GO!
Using billets to gain inside information

PURPOSE: To practise inner communication while removing uncertainty.

PREPARATION: All you need are a few minutes, a number of small strips of blank paper (they must be the same colour and size), and your journal or a pad of paper upon which to note your responses.

STEPS:

1. Think of an important situation in your life about which you would like more insight. State it clearly in your mind and in your journal.

2. On one side of a blank billet write down one specific aspect of this situation. Continue to do this using a different strip of paper for each component until you've exhausted all the issues involved.

3. Then fold each billet in half and then in half again. Be sure to keep the written words inside the fold, and fold each billet in the same way.

4. Place all the folded billets in a basket or bowl. Toss them around (like a salad) so it will be impossible for you to determine which is which.

5. After you have jumbled up all the billets, write a number on each one, on the outside.

6. Sit quietly with your journal or pad of paper in your lap and take a few deep, cleansing breaths.

7. Take one billet from the bowl and place it in your left hand, keeping it folded. As you close your hand around the billet, close your eyes and go inwards.

8. In your journal write down the number of the billet and note every feeling and perception you have while holding it. Call the presence of your spirit and open yourself to perceive anything and everything – images, symbols (even if fragmented), colours, even temperatures and emotions.

   Be as synaesthetic as possible, describing your perceptions from every sense. Trust everything; even the most seemingly inconsequential and fleeting 'picture' can provide a significant message.

9. After a few minutes (that's all it takes) of noting your perceptions, put that billet aside. Don't unfold it or try to determine what's written on the inside. Pick a new billet from the bowl and repeat step 8. Do this with each billet, being sure not to accidentally unfold any in the process. (There are no accidents!)

10. Once you are finished with all of the billets, open them and match each one to the numbered entries you made in your journal. Take a look at what you perceived with each facet of your situation and interpret the possible meanings. As with all intuitive symbols, if something's unclear, continue to refer to it in your journal so that a greater understanding can evolve over time.

OBSERVATION: You can also use this billet exercise to discover information about a number of different topics at the same time.
For instance, you can simply give each blank billet a different title (my job, my relationship with my children, my education, and so on). Using this billet method you will be able to get an intuitive (and impartial) overview of all the important areas of your life. In addition, you can use this process to help you make decisions, by listing one option on each billet.

You can also use this method to receive intuitive feedback about and for your friends. Simply put their names on the billets and see what images, feelings and symbols you perceive for each of them individually.

THE NEXT STEP: If you would like an extended 'read' on certain options or situations, you can put each individual billet into a sealed envelope. Number the outside of each and proceed with steps 8 and 9 as you did with the folded billets. This time, though, when you set them aside, leave them in the envelopes for several days or even a week. Then, without looking at the previous journal entry of your intuitive perceptions, do the entire process again on a different day. If you do this a number of times over several weeks, you may well discover much intuitive information and many layers of meanings as well.

14

The Road to Success

Success in intuitive development involves the same activities and attitudes that are necessary for success in life. In this chapter we will look first at some of the activities needed for success and then consider the attitudes required, as well. Finally, we will probe the deeper meanings of failure and success – opposite sides of the coin by which many of us measure our worth.

Successful Moments

Significant events, such as winning an Oscar or an Olympic gold medal, are often taken as the hallmarks of success. Yet the true nature of success is that it is created and known in the minor, and sometimes mundane, activities in life. As Scott Hamilton, 1984 gold medallist for figure skating, would probably be the first to tell you, as great as an Olympic medal was, it was little compared with what he achieved later in his successful battle with testicular cancer.

Neither of these great successes occurred for Scott in one moment or even in a single event – not even his gold medal performance. His Olympic success came with every hour of practice, every meeting with choreographers and coaches, and every practice jump (whether he landed well or fell). He lived his healing success through hours and months of treatments and side-effects, and through persistent efforts in nutrition and other daily practices to support his continued well-being.

> *To achieve the success of your dreams,*
> *you have to live it every day. Success can*
> *only happen in small repeated steps –*
> *one step at a time, one day at a time.*

Here, then, are some of the daily steps you can take to enjoy the utter success of knowing your spirit.

Daily Habits for Successful Intuition

I know I've said it before, but it can't be said too often: *Learn to meditate and practise it every day*. Meditation doesn't require you to sit in a lotus position and chant. It merely helps you build the discipline of stilling the mind and going inwards for your source of strength and information. It lifts your consciousness to a higher, more tolerant and self-aware perspective. And, at the very least, meditating regularly relaxes the body and minimises stress. So get a few guided imagery tapes and give it a try. Make a long-term commitment so you can see (and benefit from) the long-term results!

Check in with your intuitive source every day. This will, of course, be part of your meditations, but also check in every day at other times as well. When you wake up, ask your intuition what your lesson or message is for that day. Simply 'look' for one image and then go back to that image when you go to bed – just to see how that message applied to your day.

Practise with imagery and the visualisation of symbols. Write thorough descriptions of dream and meditation images in your journal, even filling in the missing spaces with what you imagine might be there. Practise your skills of observation, and learn to look at all images and symbols (either internal or in your environment) from all sides and from all perspectives.

Carry a small notebook or journal with you so that you can write down your intuitive hunches every day. Note the impressions you perceive spontaneously, and record them as they occur to you. Note what they are, when and where you were, and how you felt. It may seem like a burden to be jotting down notes to yourself throughout your day, but it will take only a little time if you keep it brief, just a few key words. This notebook is not only for your intuitive messages but also for your feelings, observations, ideas, and even new words and jokes. This exercise helps you to: heighten your powers of observation; live with a higher understanding of your feelings and your motivations; and become more aware of how you direct your mental energies. Most of all, it causes you to listen more attentively to all of the talk that goes on in your head, giving you more freedom to choose thoughts that nourish your creativity and spirit rather than those that lower your experience of curiosity and strength.

Keep a dream journal. Your dreams can give you guidance in many more ways than just intuitively. Your dreams can tell you about your emotions, your history, your unconscious, your hopes, your fears and your wishes. Your dreams help you get to know better all the different parts of yourself, and they help you learn more about your own personal symbols and about interpreting symbols in general. In order to know your dreams better, you first have to remember them. So keep a notebook next to your bed and write your dreams in it as soon as you wake up. If your dreams fade quickly, try to write a few words down even before you sit up (this really works!). If you have no memory of a dream, note the first feelings and ideas in your mind when you wake up. Before too long you will be remembering your dreams in detail and enjoying the self-discovery and insight they can provide.

BREAK THROUGH

Tonight before you go to bed, ask your spirit any question that you have about yourself or your life. Write it down at the top of a blank journal page and affirm, as you are falling asleep, that you will know more about this through the night. Jot down any images or dreams, even if they don't make sense, whenever you wake up (throughout the night or in the morning). Also, note your feelings and any further questions that these insights might trigger. Use this process whenever you want to point your dreams towards discovery!

Attitudes and Ideals that Promote Success

1. Emotional consistency, self-love, tolerance and forgiveness of others. (Remember, blame diminishes your power.)

2. Physical activities that honour you (such as exercise and relaxation), and changing those that don't.

3. Patience with yourself and others. This includes faith in your skills, courage to take risks, and permission to make mistakes (and not judge yourself harshly for them).

4. Commitment without fixating on the outcome. Act every day on every intention you hold.

5. Appreciation for what you have and, most importantly, for who you are and for the effort you make to live your truth.

6. Mental calm with an air of curiosity, discovery and wonder.

7. Trust instead of worry. Trust not only in the guidance provided by your intuition, but also in yourself, your life and your world.

Trust: the Alpha and Omega of Success

Very early in this book I emphasised the absolute necessity of trust for a successful experience of intuition. That, above any other single factor, is the key. Time and time again I have seen people deny their intuitive experience because of an inability to trust. Everybody is intuitive – everybody. Some people may be more intuitive initially, simply because they have greater trust in themselves.

Yet intuition is just one tiny part of life which is influenced in this way. Indeed, whether or not you experience anxiety and worry or peace of mind will be entirely dependent upon your determination to trust.

> *Peace is the absence of worry.*
> *Worry is the absence of trust.*

In any given moment we can choose to worry about a situation – any situation, small or large – or we can choose to trust that the same situation will unfold as it should. Trust is a choice, as is worry. (And if you say you can't help worrying, don't kid yourself, your thoughts are always your choice.)

The choice to worry is quite literally a decision to obsess about an outcome. And once you make that choice, you will actively be creating struggle in your life. The action you take with any worrisome task becomes filled with anxiety. And the more you worry, the harder the task becomes.

Like most of us, my son, Devin, has two ways of doing his work (homework in his case): the hard way and the easy way. He and his cousins recently returned from a skiing holiday with their grandmother. (My mother, now almost 80, skis the most difficult slopes in the Rocky Mountains, plays tennis four times a week and plays the piano professionally – not for the money, but because she loves it. She never says 'no' to her spirit!)

Having missed school, Devin had an enormous amount of work to complete. Every night for over a week he would spend hours pacing from room to room lamenting, 'I can't do my home-work; I can't do my homework!' Though he could usually do an entire maths assignment in minutes, it was now taking him hours. The amount of work was occupying his mind more than the actual work itself. My advice to take things one step at a time, to stop focusing on the worry, did not help. Even my attempts to provide incentives were unsuccessful.

The following weekend we were watching the Winter Olympics (a big event throughout my life since I grew up in a skiing family). Scott Hamilton, now also a sports commentator, was talking about what it took to win a medal in his sport. 'I know it sounds silly,' he said, 'but you have to skate stupid. You have to get out of your head and trust that your body knows what it needs to do. If you're skating smart, that means you're spending all of your time thinking. If you're busy thinking about what you're supposed to do, you're not *doing* what you're sup-posed to do!' With that, my son turned to me and said, 'Mom, that's what I've been doing all week! I've been *thinking* about my homework instead of *doing* my homework!'

This little story is important in two ways. It shows, as we have already seen, that over-analysis can impede the experience of trust. But, more importantly, it illustrates how easily we can create our own hardships and obstacles. (It also illustrates how kids can accept wisdom from others before they can from their mothers!) Excessive thought can turn into fixation and is only one step away from worry. And this type of thought process can create some of the greatest difficulties in our lives.

Believing that you will not be able to complete a task will either prevent you from doing it altogether or cause you enor-mous struggle while completing it. *Trusting* that you will complete a task will remove the experience of hardship from that activity – whether it is a two-minute skating programme, two weeks of homework or several years of study at university. Trusting won't change the task itself, but it will change your def-inition of that task from struggle to mere effort. And it will allow you to take action without anxiety.

BREAK THROUGH

Think about a long-term activity that you continnously experience as a struggle. Since it takes time and exposure to alter an established thought pattern, choose something to which you will be exposed over time. Consider how you have struggled over it, how you feel when you have to take it up again, even how you feel when you think about it. Take a moment now to create a simple statement of trust about your ability to do this activity successfully. For instance, 'I trust that I can handle this project with ease and grace.' Or 'I trust that every aspect of this situation will turn out as it should.' Write your trust affirmation (naming the specific situation) on a card to use every day. From now on, say this affirmation *every time* you think about this activity. Close your eyes and visualise yourself taking this action easily. Do not allow yourself to engage in worry or to ruminate about how miserable this task (or relationship or situation) is going to be for you. Just use your affirmation of trust and release the worry every single time that it starts to fill your mind.

Without trust even your thinking becomes filled with anxiety. Your life becomes a long series of concerns which you are perpetually reinforcing. 'Is this project going to work? What if I don't get the job? Does he/she love me enough to stay?' and so on. The depth of your worry will literally be determined by how much airtime you give each question in your head. If you trust that you will be with the right partner in your life, you won't have to worry about your partner leaving. If you trust that the career you are supposed to have will come to you, you don't have to worry about your job interview. If you trust that you are capable of pursuing *any* purpose, then you don't have to worry about the project you choose to embrace. Do you see the pattern in these examples? The words in each sentence?

If you trust, then you don't have to worry!

How Can I tell if I Have Arrived (at Being Intuitive)?

Arriving at the goal of being intuitive is rather like arriving at being creative. You don't arrive by being it. You arrive by *doing it*!

If you have begun to look towards your inner guidance frequently throughout your day, then you have arrived. If you live consciously and seek a greater understanding of yourself and where you are going, then you have arrived. If you have found a new joy and a sense of wonder in the discovery of who you are, then you have arrived. If you are seeing your life through the eyes of your spirit, then you have arrived.

Taking action to find your spirit is what you need to do to be intuitive. This book tells you how to take that action, but your life tells you whether or not you have made that action a habit. Let's take a look.

Signs That You Are Successfully Listening to Your Spirit

Do you feel a greater sense of purpose in your life, even if that purpose takes you in a difficult direction?
If you feel that every single day has provided some experience of meeting your purpose, then you have engaged your intuitive mind. Those who don't listen to their intuition often don't feel they have a purpose or don't know what their purpose is.

Do you live with clarity?

Clarity is a natural byproduct of listening to your intuition. Decision-making and your understanding of people and events become clearer and more insightful when you're intuitive. People who don't listen to their intuition tend to live in a perpetual state of confusion – stumbling around a labyrinth made up of the same circuitous thoughts they've been thinking their whole life. They can often take years to make important life decisions.

Do you feel that your life is relatively struggle-free?

Remember, struggle-free does not mean effortless. There are certainly going to be challenges, but these will be challenges that support your purpose, and you will meet them with intention and even enthusiasm. For those who don't make listening a habit, life can be a struggle – in fact, an ongoing series of struggles! For these people, going to work is a trial; keeping the house organised is a problem; returning calls, doing chores, and even interacting with others can be hardships. Their experience of enthusiasm is a distant memory, stored in the back of the cupboard with the empty luggage waiting to come out only for holidays and some weekends.

Do you determine your own course of action regardless of what others think?

Listening to your spirit (and trusting that part of yourself) not only puts you in the driver's seat, but it puts you there with confidence. People who don't listen to themselves don't believe in themselves. They base their decisions – from their choice of car to their kids' clothes – on what others are going to think of them. Sometimes they will go out of their way to do things for other people in order to get their approval. Helping others is a great thing unless you do so because you can't feel good about yourself otherwise.

Do you spend more time thinking about your truth than your image?
Listening inside requires a daily habit of looking for a deeper understanding of yourself and your world, instead of looking merely at the surface. Those who don't make inner listening a habit often have a habit of inner talking. If their minds aren't aware of their spirit, they are often filled with ego – telling themselves how much better or how much worse they are than other people. (And sometimes they do even both!) Those who listen define themselves as spirit and wouldn't spend time or energy describing themselves in ways that don't fit that definition.

Do you design your life in a way that honours you? In other words:

- Do you take real action on your dreams every day?
- Are you organised enough not to waste time looking for things and repeating unnecessary steps?
- Do you say 'no' when you want to say 'no'?
- Do you give yourself permission to do what you can do in a day, not what you should do in a day?
- Do you take time for yourself every day – physical time, creative time and inward relaxing time?

These are the ways to design a self-honouring life. Those who don't listen to their spirit don't take time for themselves or their dreams. They are too busy doing what they 'should' do for a 'perfect' life, sacrificing their time to the demands of their 'expectations' and to their own disorganisation. Lots of people have a demanding life. Those who listen demand that they bring their spirit with them.

When something doesn't work out in your life, do you find the gift in it?
This is a big one – even for people who listen to their spirit every

day. When things don't go the way you expect or you don't achieve the results you hoped for, there can be lots of disappointment. But, disappointment notwithstanding, those who listen will seek to understand a greater meaning in the experience. They will look for the gift, for the benefit that can be gained. Those who don't listen to (or look for) their inner guidance will be thrown into a state of depression and feel victimised. They will blame themselves and/or others for their misfortune. And the only thing they will learn from the experience is that 'things never work out' for them.

Do you spend part of your life in service to others?

A life of service is a reflection of inner listening. This service can be through your work or in your personal life, to your children or to the community, in ways small or large. When you listen to your spirit, it almost inevitably leads you – in some part of your life – to service. This service does not require that you sacrifice yourself or that you do other people's work for them. Indeed, the greatest service you can provide is to help others discover their own strengths and gifts. So, service to your children doesn't involve making their beds or doing their laundry but teaching them to make their beds and do their laundry! When you listen, your spirit can show you opportunities for service in some very unexpected places.

I am reminded of the story of Bismarck during the Franco-German War. After many tense hours, a very difficult battle was won and he could relax a little. He took out a cigar, and a wounded soldier nearby began looking longingly at it. Without hesitation Bismarck lit the cigar and gave it to the soldier, who appreciated it greatly. Bismarck later commented, 'It was the best cigar I ever had!'

While service can be giving away a cigar, it is not giving away your life. Remember, giving *of* yourself doesn't mean giving *up* yourself. Take another look at Part II and maintain the balance between service and self-honouring.

Do you enjoy your own company and appreciate not only the things you do for yourself, but also the things you do *with* yourself?

People who listen inside learn to love who they are. It means that the spirit you regard as your source of guidance is also your source of love. You *are* your best friend, and you are rarely bored!

Do you recognise where you are perfect?

Perfection is an internal experience not external. People who engage their spirit have an enormous tolerance for the apparent imperfections in their lives and in others. They have great patience for plans working out in their own time. People who don't engage their spirit are forever struggling to make things outside themselves perfect, because that is the only place where they can define perfection. Often they feel bad about themselves when they can't make a perfect world. Let's take a closer look at this thing called perfection.

Where Art Thou, Perfection?

Okay, what on earth does perfection have to do with intuition, with knowing your spirit mind? It's easy:

Your spirit is your perfection!

So many people go through life defining their success through their marriages; their corporate or financial positions; their perfect homes, kids, clothes and jobs. And if any of these fall short, they see this as another opportunity to divide self from spirit by judging themselves a failure.

Please understand, this doesn't mean that if you have a neat house, you are perfection-driven. My friends say I have a 'perfect' house, but that's because I hate wasting time looking for things, so I'm very organised. I'm also very visual, as you might have guessed, and I enjoy pretty things.

Yet, the *need* for perfection is not found in your home or your job performance, or your clothes or cars. It is reflected in your attitude and behaviour relating to these things. Do you spend more time cleaning your kids' rooms than playing or talking with your kids? Do you buy a sports car because you love to drive it or because of the way it looks and what it might say about you? Do you work ninety hours a week to get a partnership in a law firm and spend no time deepening your partnership with your spouse, your kids or your spirit? Do you need the 'perfect' life to feel okay? When things aren't perfect, do you feel bad about yourself?

> *The need for perfection* outside *yourself*
> *indicates that you are unaware of the*
> *perfection* inside *yourself.*

People who are obsessed with having the perfect home, kids, job, etc. are really saying they need control. They need to exert defining influence outside themselves because they don't feel it inside themselves.

Perfectionism breeds control. But this type of control does not mean internal control (of your emotions, temper, behaviour, etc.), which I would rather call *choice*. Here we're talking about outer control (of other people, events, the environment), which I like to call *impossible!*

For most perfectionists there is a sense of something missing, a sense of emptiness and a lack of inner purpose. They are constantly, urgently and literally reaching into their environment in an attempt to define themselves through it and find what's missing.

The need for control outside yourself is expressed either through perfectionism in things or through making other people fit your agenda (which is still *your* plan for perfection). This control becomes your sole purpose. When you feel emptiness *inside* you, you will do anything and everything to fill that hole with a purpose *outside* you. But here's a secret about control:

The need for external control
always covers up panic!

Urgently trying to control the externals in your life is a sign
that deep inside you are panic-stricken. You fear that these
externals will somehow reflect the lack you are already feeling.
You are trying to hide that lack from everyone (and, most
importantly, from yourself) by creating the appearance of
fullness in the things around you – a perfect home, job and
life. These are the structures through which you define
yourself and your success. They give you purpose and keep
you from being with your internal emptiness. Who would you
become without these defining structures? How would your
well-being bear up under your own scrutiny? What purpose
would fill your life if you lost that 'perfect' job or if you weren't
busy running hither and thither making everything 'right'?
Could you still be a success if you weren't an executive, a
mother, a poet, a counsellor, a lawyer?

There is a backward logic to the need to be in control. First,
you fear that you will lose the happiness or success provided
by a defining structure in your life. So in order to feel safe, you
clutch it and control it. Consequently, you mentally link
control with safety. You believe that the more you control life,
the more harmonious and stress free it will be. But in truth,
your need for control is motivated only by your *lack* of safety.
The tighter you hold on to the externals, the more you reveal
your fear and lack of inner purpose. So don't fool yourself that
control equals harmony. Nothing could be further from the
truth. Indeed, *letting go* of the need for control creates
harmony!

But what can you do about perfection and control? First,
realise that control of the outside world is impossible. Replace
control with trust. And trust that you can be shown – in any circumstance – an opportunity to know and share your real
perfection.

Second, be clear about your intentions. In her book about relationships, *Secrets of Attraction*, my sister, Sandra Taylor, speaks of the need for this clarity in romance: 'Be careful; your purpose in pursing a romance may have other underlying unhealthy intentions ... It may be intended to win the approval of others or to ensure personal or financial security. *These intentions are fear-based and they contaminate your desire* ... Real love – and every other good thing – can be poisoned by fear. This is why it's important to look very closely at the *energy and intentions* behind every desire.' So, determine whether the intentions you hold reflect those of your spirit.

Third, stop defining yourself, your value and your purpose through people and things outside you. Sure, you can still hold the purpose of being a nurse, a pilot, an executive or a father – and you can be great at any of these. Yet, it is essential to find your purpose and perfection inside yourself first, because some day you are going to retire and your kids are going to grow up and move out. Don't wait until things are gone to discover that you've defined yourself through the temporary. Here's my motto about the temporary world:

Perfection doesn't exist.
You just have to be perfect without it!

So find your perfection where it really lives, inside you. It is the natural state of your spirit. And your excellence requires nothing more of you than embracing that spirit in everything you do. You may not know what your purpose is because you've been camouflaging it in your environment for too long. Using your own processes and the steps outlined in this book, you can get to know your spirit. Then your inner guidance will show you the way, and you can't help but succeed!

Are You Failing to Recognise Your Success?

Excluding specific situations or events outside your realm of influence – such as winning the lottery or losing a court case – there are very few real failures. If you seem to be experiencing persistent failure (either in your personal life or with your career), I suggest that you have not failed at all but have succeeded absolutely!

You have never been a failure at becoming what you believe you can become. *Now, it is true that you can fail at getting what you want. But it is impossible to fail at becoming who you believe yourself to be.* This may seem a little confusing at first, but let's look at success and failure to see what this all means.

Success and failure – regardless of how you define them – are both outcomes of your actions and beliefs. And whether those outcomes increase your wealth and reputation or diminish them, they are still outcomes that you *created.* You are responsible for creating the reality you are living now. You had a thought, you took an action, you had another thought, you took another action. And with time *you succeeded* in turning all of that thought and effort into the precise outcome which those thoughts defined.

See how powerful you are? You can make or break *yourself* just by the beliefs you hold and how you follow up on them. I bet you didn't know that you have been succeeding all your life, did you? As a matter of fact, everyone has.

Everyone has succeeded in becoming who they believe themselves to be. For example, if you believe that you are secretary material and you become a secretary, then you have succeeded. If you believe that you can own your own company and you have taken steps to do that, then you have succeeded. If you believe that you are a failure and you've lost three jobs in three years, then you have succeeded. If you believe that you will never reduce your mountain of debt and your charges keep growing, then you have succeeded! These are all success stories!

Your life is a success story! It is utterly important that you understand this successful history if you want to change the future.

You cannot change your ability to create
what you want until you recognise your
success in creating what you already have!

If you know you have succeeded in making your beliefs real (no matter what those beliefs are), then all you have to do is change your thinking and the actions you take in order to make a new kind of success. Be aware that changing your belief system doesn't happen overnight. But it can happen over time – through affirmations, writing in your journal, and with conscious effort. By reaching out for your spirit, you can change old belief patterns of lack to those of self-esteem, worth and absolute potential.

BREAK THROUGH

Think of an obstacle to success that you've been experiencing in your life. It could be a belief, a fear, a feeling, anything. Decide what it is and give it substance. In your imaging make it real. Turn it into a physical object – a structure, an animal, a thing. Close your eyes and picture it in front of you. Notice how you feel. Learn everything you can about this obstacle. What and who places it before you? Does it reflect a part of yourself? Take a moment to *become* that structure. Go inside it. Breathe it, and reassess it from this new perspective. Know this obstacle from the inside out. What do *you* do to perpetuate this obstacle? What can it teach you to help instead of hinder you?

Don't fall prey to sabotaging thoughts that reinforce your intention to fail. There are plenty of great ways to sabotage, such as believing that you are being held back by circumstances or by other people. Or you may feel that your friends, your spouse or your relatives will not like it if you are more successful than they are. These are just excuses which permit your continued failure by pointing to an outside reason for it. These excuses allow you to blame other people or external circumstances and not take responsibility yourself.

If you don't own responsibility for your success, then it is not your fault that you failed and it's not your job to succeed! You can stay in the familiar comfort zone of lack. You can continue to wonder what's wrong with you and why the universe doesn't let you get ahead.

And worrying about your friends' discomfort with your success only supports the negative belief that good things are bad, and bad things are normal. Unfortunately, this seems to be a common misconception in the world. I'm sure you have heard the saying, 'This is too good to be true' many times. But how often have you heard it said, 'This is too *bad* to be true'?

So show your friends and yourself how easily good thoughts and good efforts can make a great life! It is a gift you give to the whole world. For when you act with a strong belief that you are capable and determined, you mirror those qualities back to your friends. That gives them a greater opportunity to find the same strength and perseverance in themselves. Those who cannot recognise this truth and continue to diminish your success with criticism should be relegated to your past – along with toxic thought patterns and defeating behaviours. If misery loves company, let your 'friends' find their company elsewhere, because you're *not* choosing misery anymore!

BREAK THROUGH

You have an opportunity right now to change history! Take a moment to think about all the little actions you took throughout your day yesterday. Choose one action or even one thought that reflected a moment of failure or self-defeat. Close your eyes and visualise that moment. See yourself as you chose that sabotaging action or that negative thought. Now rewind the image. Take it back to the beginning and run it again. Only this time think your truth and act on your purpose. Watch yourself make the choice that honours you in thought and deed. Picture clearly this new affirming action. Anchor the image in your mind. And commit to recreating this success the next time this precise opportunity presents itself. Do this process frequently to find the many little ways you can choose a new success.

Now is the time to reconsider the concepts of 'failure' and 'success' in your life. *Recognise how successful you are and always have been at creating the reality that reflects your beliefs.* Learn about the potential of your power and confidence. Be aware that every thought you have and every step you take builds up one by one on top of each other. But the best measure of your success is in each individual moment. Are you in this moment living your truth? If so, you cannot reach a greater success. And if not, it takes only the next moment to change! Stop defining your life as success or failure and recognise it as a state of perpetual opportunity!

15

Being and Becoming

I enjoy life more now that I'm older and realise how delicate is our existence, but my intuition tells me that a new horizon will envelop me and mine into an eternal bliss.

— Robert Goulet

Robert Goulet, one of the truly great voices in American theatre and cinema, says that his intuition was stilted by his religious upbringing. Learning to trust others before himself, he fell victim to those who would lie and steal and take advantage of his kindness. In spite of this, he took the chances he needed to give his spirit a voice. (And what a voice he gave to the world!) In the above quote he shows us how his intuition has pointed the way to an eternal reality of bliss. And this is exactly what becoming is all about.

The act of 'becoming' implies developing into something new. But it actually takes you to who you already are inside (though who you are deep inside may be new to you). And it is discovery of who you have been forever (your spirit) that your becoming is all about.

The first, and perhaps largest, step on the path of becoming is going to your intuition to discover what you know. It is no coincidence that the word divine, as a verb, means 'to discover intuitively' or 'to find out by keen understanding'. But as an adjective divine means 'belonging to God'. Isn't it great that your source in understanding is also your source in the Divine? Consequently, going to your intuition is much more than about getting answers. It's about going home.

There may be nothing in life more liberating than knowing the spirit (or the soul), because that means discovering what the soul knows – about immortality, pain, love, grief, forgiveness, conflict, morality and life. Most of all, knowing the spirit means knowing a world and a life without fear. For the perspective of the soul brings with it the perspective of invulnerability and imperishability. At long last, you have the choice to make decisions and to choose pursuits solely for the richness and joy they bring rather than acting out of need, urgency or intimidation.

BREAK THROUGH

Your personal self is at a summit meeting with two of the most powerful people in the world – your spirit and that personality whom you experience as the divine being. You are seated in a small circle facing each other. Take a moment to ask your spirit and this divine being any question about any situation. Close your eyes and allow yourself to receive (and trust) any image. Also, take a moment to simply be with the love, confidence and wisdom that these two eternal and gentle beings share with you now.

This is what awaits you in the experience of becoming. What a gift it is to know that this is who you already are! And all you have to do is *remember*. You may have lost sight of it but your spirit is always there – and remembering it completely is just a few steps away.

Steps in Becoming

1. Forget any misconceptions that you are limited. Recognise that all you need is inside you. Don't link your happiness, success or well-being to events or people around you.

2. Notice those moments when you find yourself in adversarial situations (either as the victim or the winner). Challenge yourself to handle them with greater tolerance and wisdom. Don't forget that in every moment you can choose to perceive connectedness or divisiveness.

3. Stay on purpose. Every day do something that helps you discover it and live it.

4. Trust that everything that comes to you is part of the process and the plan. Know that there is something to learn in this very moment.

5. Detach – not just for detachment's sake (to relieve stress, anxiety and urgency) but for a growing and consistent awareness that your life is yours eternally. This moment is one moment out of millions. This goal is one goal in a thousand goals. This relationship is one of the hundreds of relationships you will have and have had with others on your eternal journey. Take a deep breath and relax. Knowing who you are in this *eternal* moment is more important than anything you could ever do or anyone you could ever be in the temporal 'moment'.

6. Live with integrity. That means know your truth and live your truth with every part of who you are.

Integrity Requires Integration

Choosing the path of becoming involves all these steps. These are the actions that help you know your spirit first hand. But living with integrity also requires knowing your personality and its needs and motivations. *Your integrity calls you to integrate the many layers of who you are.*

Becoming the spirit who you have been forever doesn't mean you stop being human. Disregarding any aspect of the self can send a very dangerous message of rejection to your subconscious, a rejection that diminishes your value and sabotages your success. Learning to listen to the voice of your body and the expression of your emotions (past or present, conscious or unconscious) is part of the growth that opens the gate to a new mind and a new communion with your spirit.

BREAK THROUGH

Write for five minutes in a stream of consciousness. Write about your hopes, your goals, your dreams. Don't stop. Don't think. Don't take a break. Let everything come up – your fears, your worries, your thoughts of self. Lose control of your words. Don't make sense, just make ideas. When you are done, take a look at everything that you are: dark and light; happy and sad. Don't analyse. Don't judge. Just accept and embrace every part of you. And thank yourself for making the effort to know yourself better.

It is as important to know and understand what motivates you from 'below' as from above. That which lies just below the surface of consciousness is as much a part of you as the spirit who guides you to a higher awareness. When you open to a greater spiritual reality, take care that you do not fall into the trap of holding a diminished value of your physical and emotional truths. This is a common misconception, because a new door that takes us to a greater sense of joy, power and self-actualisation may well narrow our focus on other involvements. But over time such single-mindedness can turn into a denial of the physical and emotional bodies. Never forget:

Integration of all worlds and self-knowing at all levels brings you to the greatest realisation of your truth.

So stay in the moment and stay conscious of integrating all of the worlds in which you live. *Always act on your becoming, but don't let that becoming mean that you spend your life hurtling towards something more important than who you already are now.* That is not a message you want to give yourself, because it diminishes everything about who you are now.

Don't be afraid that the integration of your spirit with your personality will inhibit your complete becoming. True becoming allows you to see, to know and to embrace all parts of yourself from the highest wisdom possible. It can allow you to be human and still show you the way to choose the highest road or the most exalted position, in any challenge and in every situation.

Taking the High Road

Throughout history and in all civilisations, humankind has known divisiveness – between the tolerant and the intolerant, between the loving and the lacking, between the spirit and the ego. In any given moment, whether collectively or individually, we can choose the high road or the low. The holocaust of the Second World War may arguably have been the most divisive action in all human history. It seemed the high road and low road were never further apart. Discovering your spirit in those conditions would seem almost impossible. Yet, I would like to share a story which illustrates that choosing the high road is never impossible – even in the lowest of times.

The story concerns a woman who, after losing her entire family in the German concentration camps, devoted herself to the care of children who were injured or left infirm by the war. Oddly, though, she chose only German children, children of the very race who killed her family and her people. She asked herself, 'What is the highest position I can take?' And she chose it.

In this one commitment we see the healing of victimisation through self-empowerment; the healing of anger through forgiveness; the recognition that even the worst emotional situations can bring benefit and opportunity; and the undoing of divisiveness by reaching out to others. This situation shows us the immeasurable gift of grace that can be received by all when, even in the worst situations, we choose to take the 'highest position' possible.

BREAK THROUGH

Think of a situation in which it is hard to feel your spirit's perspective, where the low road is the first response you lean towards. Close your eyes and leave your emotions behind for a minute. Ask yourself, 'What is the highest position I can hold in this situation?' Consider at least one possibility of a more exalted attitude or a greater action which you can take.

Take a moment to picture yourself holding this position. Every time this situation presents itself or comes to mind – even if it makes you angry or sad – ask yourself, 'What is the highest position I can take?' And know that this option is your greatest opportunity for grace. Choose it for yourself. This is the way to turn a dark situation into light!

The act of becoming requires nothing more than knowing in this very moment who you have been forever. If you know that, then you cannot help but choose the highest position; you cannot help but see events from a broader perspective; you cannot help but find the exalted joy and power inside you; and you cannot help but recognise this truth in everyone else – whether they recognise it in themselves or not. What could the world be, if each of us made this choice?

A billion stars go
spinning through the night,
Blazing high above your head.
But IN you is the presence that
will be, when all the stars
are dead.

– Rainer Maria Rilke[14]

* * * * *

Personal Study for Part IV

Use your journal and a calendar or diary to track your choices in self-actualisation. Refer to this worksheet frequently in order to review your growing level of *consciousness* in becoming. Make a real commitment to this discovery every day!

PHYSICAL

A. Which of your physical habits diminish your experience of vitality?

B. Which physical practices can you employ to heighten your energy and self-esteem?

C. Make a conscious effort to eradicate disempowering physical habits and replace them with activities that support physical union with your spirit. Every day that you choose a physical activity which supports your truth, mark your calendar with a 'B' for body.

EMOTIONAL

A. Which recurring emotional patterns continue to separate you from your sense of joy and well-being?

B. Without fixing blame, consider the negative emotions that are divisive in your relationships with others (from professional jealousy to fear or resentment).

C. Create an affirmation of release or forgiveness in order to let go of negative feelings when they happen. (See Appendix A for some ideas.)

D. After releasing a divisive emotion, replace it with an invitation to know the heart of your divine self.

MENTAL

A. What judgements have you made about yourself that diminish your experience of absolute potential, power and self-love?

B. Create a new affirmation, a belief founded upon your eternal reality, and repeat it several times a day in order to change your old cognition. Every day that you practise with affirmations, mark your calendar with an 'A'.

C. Even when you 'correctly' disagree with another's philosophy or behaviour, becoming judgemental diminishes your truth by defining life only by what's important in the temporary world. Create a brief affirmation that allows you to release judgement and embrace the tolerance of the eternal perspective.

INTUITIVE

A. Stay alert for those times each day when you ignore an opportunity to connect with the stirring of your intuitive mind. How often do you disregard the inner voice that speaks your highest good in any situation? How would the situation be different if you didn't disregard it?

B. Make a commitment to reverse these patterns and become more aware of your greatest consciousness. Every day that you engage your intuition, write an 'I' on your calendar.

SPIRITUAL

A. How much time do you devote to the experience of your spirit exclusively?

B. Resolve to meditate daily and consider what other processes or activities can help you engage more deeply in your truth. Every day that you devote some time to this type of inner experience (like meditation) write an 'S' for spirit on your calendar.

After three months, look back over your calendar. If 80 per cent of the days are marked with an S, I, A and B, you will be greatly surprised at the changes you have realised in your life. If 50 per

cent of your days are so marked, you will have begun to feel the
stirring of a great power and truth in yourself and in your life. If
only 20 per cent of the days indicate your life-changing efforts,
then ask yourself, 'Why don't I want to change my life? What's so
frightening about becoming a more joyful, purposeful, confident
person?' Recognise your payoff in staying the same. Then find
a bigger payoff in growing: the opportunity to reach every dream
inside you!

*   *   *   *   *

Appendix A

AFFIRMATIONS

Affirmations are simply formed statements that help you to focus on a higher truth, a clearer intention and a greater sense of well-being. We all spend a great deal of time lost in our thoughts, and if we don't live consciously many of those thoughts can be limiting and prevent a joyful and creative life. Happily, no matter how many past moments may have been difficult, the next moment is like a blank page upon which can be written a new thought, a greater action and a better life. So choose an affirmation from one of the lists below or create one for yourself. Read it frequently throughout the day and over the week. Use a different one next week. Keep *affirming* your truth to live your truth!

Affirmations for Greater Intuition

I am learning to listen to the spirit within me.

I am receptive and open to my inner guidance.

*Through the eyes of my spirit, I see my life
and my world.*

*My intuition guides me and alerts me
to the highest intention I can know.*

My spirit directs my purpose, for I am my spirit!

*I am open to recognise every little hunch
and intuitive opportunity.*

*In every situation I ask, 'What is the highest
position I can hold?' And I choose it.*

*I am conscious of how my intuition speaks to me,
and I respond to that voice immediately.*

*Every moment lifts me to a higher experience
of my soul.*

*I listen to my spirit. Through it, I am guided
to my greatness.*

*To know divine ideas, all I need to do
is go inside.*

*When something feels wrong, I stop and take
a moment to ask if there's another way.*

*Great potential lies before me, and I can see it
and live it every day.*

I believe in my intuitive perceptions, and I trust
where they lead me.

I recognise the perfection inside me,
and I look to discover it more each day.

I rely on the power of my inner senses.

I live fully when I walk hand in hand
with my spirit!

Affirmations for Healing

I can give of myself without giving up myself.

To know healing in the present I release the past.

I am open to discover the messages of my body.

I forgive myself for having allowed others to
define me.

I know myself as a divine spirit and release
attack and fear.

I release all that is toxic in my life and choose truth instead!

I trust the perfection inside me and know that everything – everything – evolves in the right way at the right time.

I express my feelings. I find healthy ways to let go of my anger and hurt.

I am conscious of my body, and I honour its needs.

I change the perspective of lack to the wisdom of love.

I release denial, and I recognise and change that which does not honour me.

I release my fears and embrace my power!

I am willing and able to act on my truth.

My feelings are the guideposts to my understanding. I know and accept them.

*I give my worries to God, and I fill my mind
with the peace of trust.*

Affirmations for Life

*I open my senses and embrace the world
with curiosity.*

*I choose relationships that honour me. I embrace
only those who reflect my value and grace.*

I value what's important, not what's urgent.

*I trust my own ideas. I am self-reliant
and confident in my truth.*

I recognise the abundant potential inside me!

*I give my spirit a voice in my life and know its
power and love in every decision and action.*

*In every moment I live to realise my full
creative potential.*

I remember who I am eternally!

*I find the beauty and the value in myself
and in everything around me.*

*I am true to myself and meet every obstacle
with a sense of discovery.*

I don't have to worry because I trust.

*I recognise the power in the little steps of my life
and choose each step accordingly.*

I take time for myself every day.

*I create a balance between my choices for others
and my choices for myself.*

*Each moment is an opportunity for peace.
I release urgency and the need to control.*

*Everything I choose reflects my truth.
I live with integrity.*

I recognise my ability to create a great life!

*I release control of the outside world and know
that my perfection lies within.*

*I make choices on my own behalf and take action
on my dreams every day.*

*I am a person of value. When I know my value,
I meet my destiny!*

*Mistakes are my teachers, and I am not afraid
to make them.*

*I can give to others and give to myself
without conflict.*

The spirit within me guides me in all endeavours.

*I look for the grace in everyone.
To see it in all is to know it in me.*

Appendix B

Key Symbols

As we have already seen, symbols can be figurative or literal, universal or personal. Below are the 'universal' interpretations for some of the more common symbols. Don't forget, in *every* symbolic experience, first ask yourself what the symbol means for you. Make a note of it in your journal so you can compile your own dictionary of symbols.

Babies: babies, new life, rebirth, enthusiasm, new purpose.

Boats: movement, travel (often near water). Sometimes, a relationship riding on the seas of emotion (in this case, the specific details will indicate the nature of the relationship: for instance, a boat tossing on stormy seas indicates a stormy relationship).

Cars (also horses, carriages and other vehicles): choices and action regarding direction in life. (Specific details of the image – going backwards, being in the driver's seat, travelling on a bumpy road – will indicate the nature of those choices.)

Chains (also shackles): restriction, constraints, immobility (often self-imposed).

Clouds (dark and foreboding): stormy and dark emotional experience; **(fluffy and light):** happiness, natural easiness, breezy personality.

Clouds or fog (above or around a person's head): confusion, inability to see things clearly, lack of direction (often self-created).

Coffins: the death or end of a situation or relationship, laying something to rest.

Concrete (also stone or steel): an unchanging condition, a fixed and inflexible person unlikely to be influenced.

Crowns: lofty or noble ideas, self-respect, satisfaction, a promotion at work or increased recognition.

Crowns (tarnished or lost): loss of self-respect, demotion or loss of a position at work, lack of self-esteem.

Fabric: nature or make-up of a person's life or relationship. The condition of the fabric – brightly coloured, torn, faded, patched, in need of repair – indicates the life or relationship condition.

Flight (also birds): freedom, ascension, mobility, travel, gathering momentum, speed, experience of the spirit; **(broken wings, caged birds):** dispiritedness, loss of freedom, heaviness, being trapped, feeling as if there are no choices.

Flowers (also gardens): joy, union or reunion, celebration, springtime or summertime, growth.

Grapes (also pumpkins): harvest, abundance. Sometimes, the completion of a task, the autumn, richness of an experience.

Halos: enlightened mind and higher spiritual thoughts, spirit guides and teachers, purification of mind.

Higher ground: advantage, gain, opportunity, strength.

Keys (also doors): opportunities, openings to new directions, new conditions. (The number of keys or doors often indicates the number of choices, or, at least, diversity.)

Lanterns (also beacons, lighthouses): illumination, direction, clarity, understanding.

Lilies (white): purity, Easter, springtime, new birth, spirituality.

Paths: direction in life, a course of action, sense of purpose and directives; **(obstructed):** inability to take action, loss of purpose or direction, hesitance to confront challenges.

Peaks, mountains: ascension to a higher perspective, an effort to raise oneself up.

Pockets (closed): stinginess, diminished resources; **(deep):** plentiful resources, accumulation; **(empty):** financial concerns; **(hands thrust deeply into):** inability to act or determination not to act, desire to withhold personal expression or participation in a certain situation.

Rabbits: fertility, gentleness.

Scales: justice, balance, equitability (in relationships, agreements or legal dealings).

Scales (tipped): injustice, victimisation, imbalance (legally, financially or personally).

Snails: slow action, deliberation, progress through small steps, perhaps too guarded for swift action.

Thrones: an individual's position or reputation (often relating to career).

Two (of anything): duality, alternatives, choices, a second unknown opportunity. Sometimes, ambivalence or indecision.

Trumpets: messages, wakening, a call to important information.

Water (pouring of): sharing and expressing of emotions and/or spirit; the integration of the emotional and the spiritual (when pouring back and forth between vessels).

Water (travelling upon or across): a trip over or near water, initiating a monumental undertaking (when crossing a large body of water), broadening one's horizons, taking a new direction or moving one's home (especially when crossing a river).

Wheat (and other grains): fertility, richness, abundance, fullness, nurturing and nourishment.

Wings: flight, exhilaration, freedom, ascension; **(broken):** debilitation, restriction of action, being earthbound or captive in personal perspective or experience.

Colours

Colour	Key Words
Red	Power, heat, speed, energy, action. Sometimes, conflict.
Orange	Warmth, regeneration, vitality, science, logic, detail.
Yellow	Healing, creativity, intellect, philosophy, joy.
Green	Balance, healing, peace, expansion, growth, abundance.
Pink (and burgundy)	Love, devotion, family, marriage, release of conflict.
Blue (and indigo)	Communication, spirituality, calm, psychic powers, clairvoyance, intuition, clairaudience, unconditional love.
Violet/ purple	Spiritual unfolding, magic, transformation, mysticism, discipline, rituals, leadership.
Black	Meditation, detachment, karma, duty, lessons, structure, restriction.
Brown	Grounding, stability, reliability, follow-through, detail, science. Sometimes, stubbornness.
Milky white or silver	Emotions, motherhood, reflection, receptivity, psychic abilities.
Clear (or brilliant) white	Purity, power of spirit, selflessness, release of physical, clarity, penetration.

Directions

Left: Past, old patterns, history, completion.

Up: Higher mind, spirit, rest, receptivity.

Right: Future, goals and direction, creation, expression, new beginnings.

Down: Personality, physical world, activity, physical energy.

Elements

Air: Intellect, philosophy, conceptualisation, mental creativity, flight, travel, freedom, broadening horizons, dreaminess. (Colour indications: yellow, turquoise, white, sky blue.)

Earth: Grounding, detail, science, follow-through, building, structure, activities with nature, history or interest in pantheistic societies, work with the earth. (Colour indications: brown, green, light grey, rusty orange.)

Fire: Creativity, power, destruction, initiation, energy, anger, difficult or sudden change, the burning off of old conditions or emotions. (Colour indications: red, orange, yellow.)

Water: Flexibility, emotions, reflection, intuition, motherhood, relationships, psychic abilities, spirituality, communication, travel by water, fickleness, gradual change. (Colour indications: blue, indigo, blue green, silver.)

Notes

1. Michael Mok, interview with F. Scott Fitzgerald in *New York Post*, 1936.

2. Douglas Dean, John Mihalasky, Sheila Ostrander and Lynn Schroeder, *Executive ESP*, Prentice-Hall, Englewood, New Jersey, 1974, p. 169.

3. Janet Lowe, *Oprah Winfrey Speaks*, John Wiley, New York, 1998, p. 125.

4. Douglas Dean *et al.*, op. cit., p. 47.

5. Richard Wilhelm and Cary F. Baynes (trans.), *The I Ching*, Princeton University Press, 1950; p. 189.

6. Ibid, p. 179.

7. Pete Martin, interview with Alfred Hitchcock in *Saturday Evening Post*, New York, 27 July 1957.

8. Mohandas K. Gandhi, *An Autobiography*, Beacon Press, Boston, Mass., 1957, p. 193.

9. Sigmund Freud, *The Psychopathology of Everyday Life*, 1901.

10. Calvin S. Hall, *Primer of Freudian Psychology*, New American Library, New York, 1979, p. 28.

11. Paul F. Boller, Jr., *Presidential Anecdotes*, Oxford University Press, New York, 1996, p. 135.

12. Viktor E. Frankl, *Man's Search for Meaning*, Pocket Books, New York, 1963, p. 179.

13. Louisa E. Rhine, *ESP in Life and Lab*, Macmillan, New York, 1967, p. 20.

14. Stephen Mitchell (ed.), *The Enlightened Heart*, Harper & Row, New York, 1989, p. 131.

Resources

The following items are available from the author:

Healing the Darkness – a visualisation process of healing and illumination through a dialogue with the body (tape, 24 mins.)

Reading the Signs – fine tune your intuitive skills and learn how to work with the symbols of the spirit (tape, 24 mins.)

Travel into Your Past Lives – learn about the different types of karmic patterns and experience your past lives through a guided regression technique (tape: regression, 30 mins.; lecture, 30 mins.)

Speak with the Spirits – a guided meditation to help you experience your angels and spirit guides as they share their presence and consciousness with you (tape, 24 mins.)

The Magic of Gemstones and Colors – discover the fundamental qualities of colours and gems for use in healing and other metaphysical disciplines (24-page booklet)

Gemcast – a unique and easy oracle that allows you to discover your future while you learn about basic astrology and gemstones (kit including casting chart and gemstones)

To order any of the above, log on to: www.sharonklingler.com

To schedule a lecture, seminar or private consultation, telephone 440-356-9141 (USA), or write to Sharon at: P.O. Box 275, Avon, Ohio 44011, USA.

Index

They mounted their horses.

Bill still held Willy's hand. He looked down at it. She watched his face. He set his jaw. His forehead wrinkled. He grasped his pocket, held it tight a second, then said quickly, "Thanks, Miz Westall!"

"And you?" Willy said. "If I can help you?"

He made a swing into his saddle. "I might send Guillermita back," he answered.

The horses whirled. Dust fogged up.

"The corral is always waiting," Willy called.

They galloped off. Willy shut her eyes. When she looked, they had turned the corner at the bank. She leaned against the post and looked up at the sun. It was rising. A burst of yellow flooded all the sky, then it deepened into gold.

"Like S'rita's hair," she said.

"Yes, Madama," came an answer. It was Emelio at her side. He held some flowers in his hand: jasmines, crepe myrtle, and ponderosa lemon blossoms.

He handed them to her and smiled. She held them, reveling in their fragrance. Emelio thought he saw some tears.

Fanny came around the corner.

"What's the hurry?" she exclaimed. "I told 'Mara for you all to come for breakfast. I've made biscuits and here I find you at the store."

"It's a big day," Willy said. "National Guard are moving out; regular soldiers're moving in. I came down to get an early start. Don and 'Mara went to ride."

"Well, I'll be damned," Fanny said. "And here my biscuits're gettin' cold."

There came a clatter down the street. They looked up and saw a whirl of dust against the brightness, a gleam of red bandanna, then a palomino flash. Pearl was leading; Prince galloped just behind. 'Mara's hair was flying in the wind. Don whipped off his hat and waved.

"There are the children!" Willy said.

"Then let's get started, Miz Westall, for we've got an awful lot to do and the day is just beginning now."

"Yes, Fanny; we've got an awful lot to do!" Willy said.

She stood up straight. She felt very tall. She smelled the flowers in her hand, looked up at the sun, and walked back in the store.

"The day is just beginning, as you said!"

THE END